D1737556

For Danielle

Sea Otter Chiefs

(who lived in sight of Mount Fuji — on a clear day (when the rain wasn't too low or too wet!)

Mike Robinson
1996

Sea Otter Chiefs

Michael P. Robinson

Published by :

Bayeux Arts Incorporated
119 Stratton Crescent S.W.
Calgary AB, CANADA T3H 1T7

P.O. Box 586, 1 Holway Point,
Machias, Maine 04654, U.S.A.

Spantech House, Lagham Road,
South Godstone, Surrey RH9 8HB, U.K.

Design and production : George Allen and Christine Spindler
Colour photography : George Allen
Printed in Hong Kong

The publisher gratefully acknowledges the financial support of
the *Alberta Foundation for the Arts* and the *Canada Council*.

Canadian Cataloguing in Publication Data

Robinson, Mike, 1951 –
Sea Otter Chiefs

ISBN 1-896209-18-1
1. Maquinna, a Nuu-chah-nulth chief. 2. Legaik, a Tsimshian chief.
3. Cuneah, a Haida chief. 4. Indians of North America — British Columbia —
Biography. I. Title.
E78.B9R62 1995   971.1'00497   C95-910090-3

Sea Otter Chiefs

Michael P. Robinson

Table of Contents

Linguistic Note

All spellings of First Nations' words used in *Sea Otter Chiefs* are the phonetic approximations of the ships' logs and authors quoted. Where several different spellings of a word occurred, the most common form found in the historic accounts is used.

Preface

Sea Otter Chiefs is a rare book because it documents the roles and lives of three powerful chiefs of the Northwest Coast at the time of contact. Relying on the journals, diaries and notes of traders and voyageurs, as well as the stories told by contemporary local people to Marius Barbeau, the author manages to create a picture of traditional life in the 1800s which provides the reader with a sense and feel of tribal dynasties, their rituals, warfare and relationships.

This is not a new picture for contemporary scholars of Northwest Coast peoples but it does fill a gap in the literature for the specific groups. More importantly, the stories are written in a style which will appeal to descendants wanting to read their own histories, to read about their own heroes, great tradesmen and great warriors. The accounts found in the logbooks of the captains of the trade ships and travelers' diaries provide a view of highly developed nations with good trading relationships among themselves and others, mutual respect and insights into the differences of the ways people traded, made war, reconciled and feasted.

Sea Otter Chiefs also provides us with some understanding of how these great dynasties began to falter as trade increased, the area became settled and with the disruption of traditonal ritual activities by the missionaries. These remain contemporary stories the world over as traders, missionaries, settlers and those seeking to exploit local resources continue to destroy the lands and cultures of local peoples. The book provides the reader with hope, however, because anyone reading these stories about the richness of Northwest Coast cultures will have to ask, "how can they be recovered and restored?"

The link between traditional historical communities and contemporary ones remains strong as contemporary Northwest Coast peoples now continue their rituals, feasts, naming ceremonies and potlatching recovering from the long period of prohibition on these activities imposed by missionaries, police and the non-native governments. Goods are being returned by museums to communities, histories are being re-written and masks, titles and songs are being researched and reclaimed. The descendents of Cuneah, Maquinna and Legaik can thank Michael Robinson for aiding them in their tasks in their search for their own histories and cultural heroes. How fortunate that this fascinating book is being reprinted and enhanced with excellent photographs by George Allen. *Sea Otter Chiefs* is an important piece of history for each of us to enjoy.

Joan Ryan
Professor Emeritus, Anthropology, University of Calgary
Bragg Creek, Alberta, October 1995

Map of the Northwest Coast of North America c. 1800. Some 20 years after Cook's voyage, and first contact with Maquinna at Nootka Island, much of the coastline had been mapped. The villages of Maquinna, Cuneah and Legaik are highlighted.

1. Cuneah — Kiusta
2. Maquinna — Yuquot
3. Legaik — Metlakahtla

INTRODUCTION

TODAY YOU OCCASIONALLY HEAR THEIR NAMES MENTIONED IN BEER PARLOURS, ON BOARD FISH BOATS AND IN UNIVERSITY LECTURES. FOR MANY INDIAN PEOPLE OF THE NORTHWEST COAST THE SEA OTTER CHIEFS LIVE ON AS ORAL TRADITIONS AND FOLK HEROES. THEIR NAMES AND TITLES LIVE IN THE PRESENT WHILE THEIR HISTORICAL PAST IS A MATTER OF POPULAR CONJECTURE. FOR SOME REASON THE HISTORICAL RECORD OF THE NORTHWEST COAST IS OVERPOPULATED WITH SEA CAPTAINS, MISSIONARIES, COLONIAL ADMINISTRATORS AND FUR TRADERS. INDIAN CULTURE HEROES SEEM VERY RELUCTANT TO EMERGE FROM THE HISTORICAL MISTS.

We sometimes read of them when they surrendered to white culture in exemplary fashion or when they fought back with what was usually termed "barbarous" or "ungodly" behaviour. The Indian hero who was of interest to white historians was basically the hero of acculturation — the man or woman who transcended Indian culture and became a model brown white man.

Given the prejudices of the white culture historians, Indian history was left by default to the first ethnographers and anthropologists who came to the Northwest Coast. Much of the best ethnographic literature took the form of ships' logs and travellers' diaries. Many of the first white men to voyage along the Coast kept sensitive and well written accounts of what they were seeing first-

Private Collection

A SEA OTTER.

photo : British Columbia Archives and Records Service.

At left *: Prior to the arrival of the European traders, the sea otter was traditionally prized for its fine fur and its pelt was worn by high-ranking people. Almost hunted to extinction by the early nineteenth century, today the sea otter is re-establishing itself in kelp beds and along reefs off the west coast of Vancouver Island.*

The engraving of the sea otter is based on a painting by J. Webber, artist on Cook's voyage.

hand. The first anthropologists to arrive on the Coast came much later, after the fur trade had ended and the Indian cultures were in chaos and decline. Most of the social scientists valued Indian culture in itself and for itself and, in their monographs and field notes, we sometimes find mention of fine Indian heroes. Some do have a good data base to reconstruct an Indian history that will have meaning for present-day Indian people on the Coast. This will be a history of heroes who lived and died as members of societies that were being assaulted on all sides by social change that came uninvited.

The three Indian culture heroes we are about to discover made good use of the situation in which they found themselves. They lived in the later 1700s and early 1800s and, while it is unlikely that any of them ever met one another, they were talked of by the white traders and explorers up and down the coast of what is now British Columbia. They were three of the greatest chiefs of the early culture contact period, and they monopolized the sea otter trade in their districts to their own peoples' economic advantage. When we say they were chiefs, we mean that they were heads of village groups that moved about a string of winter

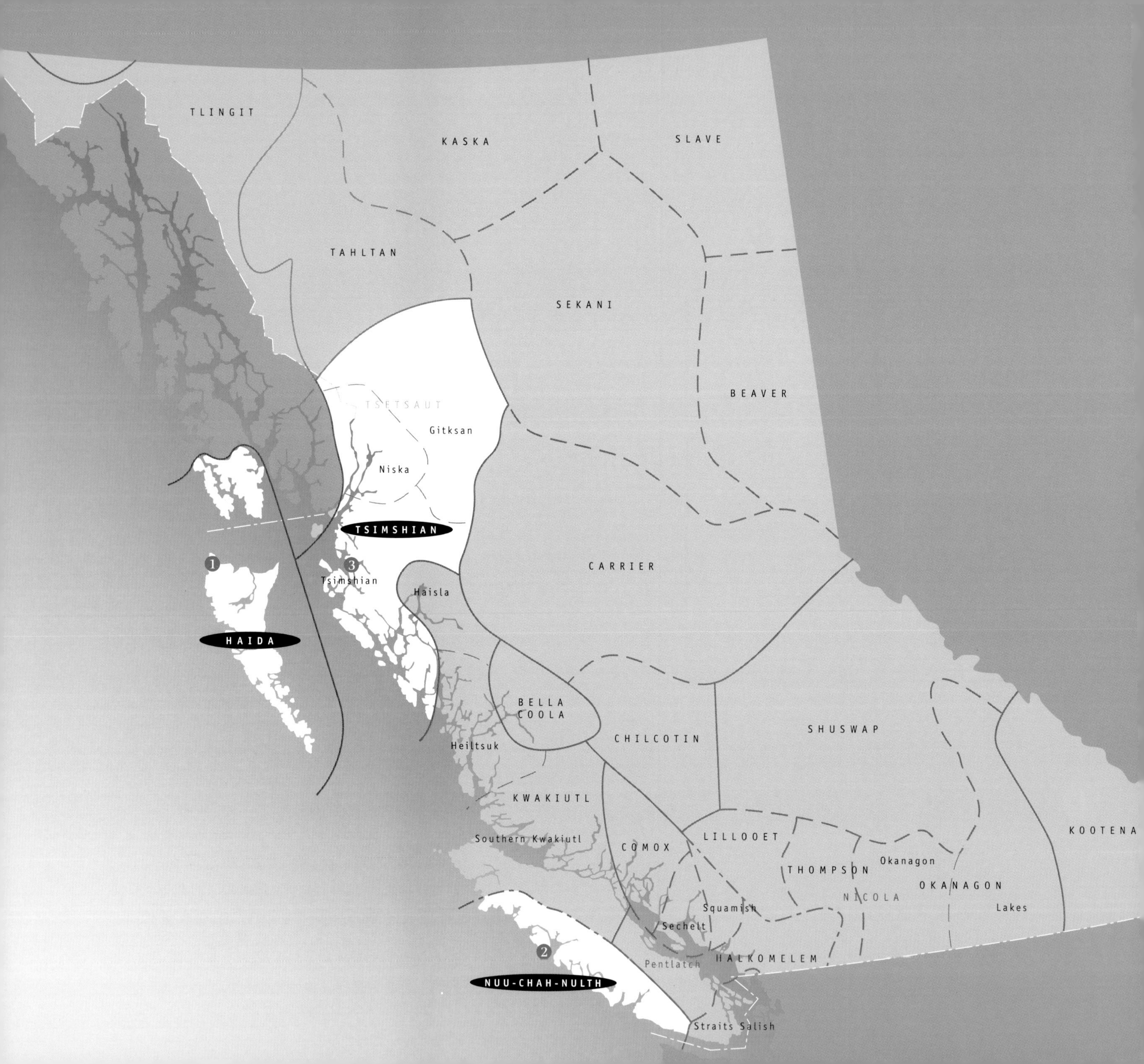
TLINGIT
KASKA
SLAVE
TAHLTAN
SEKANI
BEAVER
TSETSAUT
Gitksan
Niska
TSIMSHIAN
1
3
Tsimshian
Haisla
CARRIER
HAIDA
BELLA
COOLA
CHILCOTIN
SHUSWAP
Heiltsuk
KWAKIUTL
KOOTENA
Southern Kwakiutl
COMOX
LILLOOET
THOMPSON
Okanagon
OKANAGON
NICOLA
Lakes
Squamish
Sechelt
2
Pentlatch
HALKOMELEM
NUU-CHAH-NULTH
Straits Salish

At left *: Aboriginal language subdivisions in British Columbia. Traditional territories of the Haida, Tsimshian, and Nuu-chah-nulth people at the time of culture contact with the European traders in the late eighteenth century are highlighted. The villages of Cuneah (1), Maquinna (2), and Legaik (3) are indicated with red dots.*

and summer villages in the annual cycle of feasting, fishing, trading and gathering wild foods. In the three societies of which they were members – *Haida, Tsimshian,* and *Nuu-chah-nulth* (sometimes erroneously called *Nootka*) – there were no elected leaders or politicians. The basic unit of social organization was the family group and, beyond that, there were collections of different families who lived together, in many cases from their historical present back to myth time.

As a family's fortunes rose and fell, so did its position within the local group or village. And it is only natural that some families had more successful hunters, better fishermen and better leaders than others. As the family grew from generation to generation new houses were constructed, potlatches were given to substantiate family names and ancestral crests, and new titles and privileges evolved. Some privileges came through battle and territorial expansion, while others came via marriage and new family alliances. The latest archaeological evidence suggests that some parts of the Coast have been inhabited for 9,000 to 10,000 years. We can therefore appreciate that the societies in this area of the world had a great deal of

Mapping information – Wilson Duff

time to develop and mature before the white culture disturbance began in 1778 with the arrival of Captain Cook's three vessels in Nootka Sound.

At the moment of culture contact the long slow period of evolution came to an end. New alien social forces began to redirect the local forces at work in the Indian societies. The three men who are the subject of this research were among the first to deal with the problems and benefits of contact. They used the existing powers of their own societies to check and absorb what they wanted from the whites. They fought to maintain their people's land rights and they directed much of the sea otter trade until its economic and near physical extinction in the 1830s. By way of introduction, these men were:

Chief Cuneah of the *Kiusta* village group,
Chief Maquinna of the *Tahsis-Yuquot* village group and
Chief Legaik of the *Kispakloats* village group.

The spellings given here are the approximations developed in the logs and journals which form the base of their historical memory. While these approximate spellings convey the historical personalities, they do not in any way do justice to their correct linguistic forms.

While Chiefs Cuneah and Maquinna are well represented in the historic record, only Legaik is remembered both in the historic and anthropological records: Marius Barbeau, an anthropologist from the National Museum of Man in Ottawa, collected a considerable body of folklore of Legaik in the 1920s and 1930s. The Legaik narratives form a comprehensive base for restoring the inadequacies of the historic record.

To mention briefly the topic of political organization of Northwest Coast Indian societies, it will be useful to consider what changes the culture contact period began. We have considered the village group, comprised of several families of ordered social rank. Anthropologists and political scientists characterize village political structure as a *Chiefdom*. Inevitably as political organization moves beyond the *Tribe* (a smaller group of families living and hunting and gathering together) one family and its strongest male and female members start to exert a powerful influence over the fortunes of other families in the local village group. The small societies confronted by the first whites on the Northwest Coast were chiefdoms, and they were administered by a body of village elders under the figurehead of the chief. Chiefdoms transcend tribal society in their density of population and their more complex web of redistribution of food and wealth.

The chiefdom can be viewed by analogy as a neighbourhood serviced by a central supermarket. The village family elders and their chief functioned like the manager and executives of redistribution. While the chief was expected to make important decisions and lead action groups to hunt or to battle, he did not have a final veto. He was advised and constrained by his executive advisors who provided an important check to his unilateral power of decision. A good chief made more good decisions than bad ones — and as long as the chiefdom could effectively redistribute food resources and the necessary items of material wealth, there would be little need to challenge his authority. As long as the economic base of the chiefdom remained closed and static, there was no need to expand the services already provided. A major characteristic of Northwest Coast chiefdoms prior to contact was their incredible stability over time. The archeological record demonstrates how consistent was the tool kit of the Northwest Coast peoples. And the tool kit is a good reflection of the food resources available and their stability year in and year out. This paragon of ecological adaptation to the coastal environment was initially upset by an alien economic factor: the price Chinese merchants were willing to pay European fur traders for the sea otter pelts. In exchange for sea otter pelts, the chiefs who coordinated their gathering and sale could introduce a new economic base to their chiefdoms. Iron tools, sugar-based food, guns and sail cloth ushered in a social upheaval on a scale unrealized in 10,000 years.

Within a few years, carved masks, totem poles, house beams, canoes and household paraphernalia began to reflect the input of the iron adze and knife edge. Canoes went back and forth between villages under sail. Gunfire replaced stone weapons in battle, molasses and hard tack entered the diet, and watered down trade whiskey and rum began to heighten tensions at all social gatherings. Instead of following the yearly round of food gathering, many chiefdoms banked on the continuing availability of white food and went off on extended binges of sea otter hunting.

The old chiefdoms then began to reflect the white culture impacts in a special way: chiefs who could coordinate the largest sea otter hunts brought the greatest new economic impact to their chiefdoms. The greater the trade, the greater the amounts of new wealth that could be amassed. And, with greater wealth came greater chiefdoms — chiefdoms that became too big to administer on the old political model. Politically, the next step was proto statedom, with several chiefdoms uniting (generally through force on the part of one) to form a super-chiefdom. It appears that the sea otter chiefs were actively involved in this very process — guiding their chiefdoms into the next stage of political and economic organization to an unheard of height of power on the Northwest Coast. Any expansion of a chiefdom's redistributional boundaries occurred at the expense of neighbouring chiefdoms, and many of the old political leaders of neighbouring chiefdoms greatly resisted an expansionist neighbour. From all accounts, Mao's comment that political power grows out of the barrel of a gun held true. Musket skirmishes between competing chiefdoms often resulted in more catastrophe than expansion. The old warriors, accustomed to winning fights through their skill in combat, soon learned a new skill — avoidance of combat when the other side fought from the safety of an offshore canoe and with gunshot rather than arm muscle.

As the chiefdom expansion process became more chaotic and aggressive, the European powers took a greater interest in stabilizing Indian society. They did so out of mercantile motives, soon realizing that the very trade they had initiated was now turning against them. Articles the Indians desired in trade became victims of the new economy. When everyone had access to iron tools, then cotton clothing, mirrors, liquors and jewelry assumed new importance. When the trade attractiveness of these goods passed, the market began to go against the Europeans.

Maquinna's people in Nootka Sound wanted Monterey abalone shells to adorn their crest masks and poles. Cuneah's people wanted help in raising new poles with block and tackle, and expressed an interest in acquiring long boats with oars and sails for coastal travel. Legaik wanted umbrellas and admission to the Anglican Church — not out of a desire to acculturate, but rather to gain the spiritual power of the whites to complement the powers he already controlled.

As the pace of social and economic change grew more hectic, the fur trade began to suffer. Traders now conscripted large numbers of men to hunt fur seal and sea otter in the Aleutians as these animals dwindled in numbers on the Northwest Coast. Within the sea otter chiefs' lifetimes the boom soured and turned to bust. Introduced diseases began to take a horrendous toll on a people who had never developed defence antibodies to combat measles, smallpox and gonorrhea.

While the process of chiefdom expansion was turned around, the chiefs themselves never looked back. They continued to function socially as though a resurgence of the market might occur. One by one, unaccustomed to their fall in wealth, they died. There is good evidence to show that the names Cuneah, Maguinna and Legaik were passed on within the great families. The titles conveyed great prestige to succeeding generations and placed communal expectations upon their recipients. While the name of Cuneah seems to have fallen from use, Maguinna and Legaik are both alive today. The present chief of the Moachaht people in Nootka Sound is Mr. Ambrose Maquinna. The Legaik family name is still alive in Kitamaat village. So the spirit of the founders has been passed on to each succeeding generation.

In the next three chapters we will examine the references of ships' logs, gentleman adventurers' diaries and the Legaik narratives of Marius Barbeau to recreate the history of the sea otter chiefs. We shall see how they each guided their chiefdom's expansion and how they fought to maintain trade supremacy amongst their neighbouring chiefdoms. In essence, we will be studying great leadership in small societies, and learning about three men whose rightful place in our history has been vacant for too long.

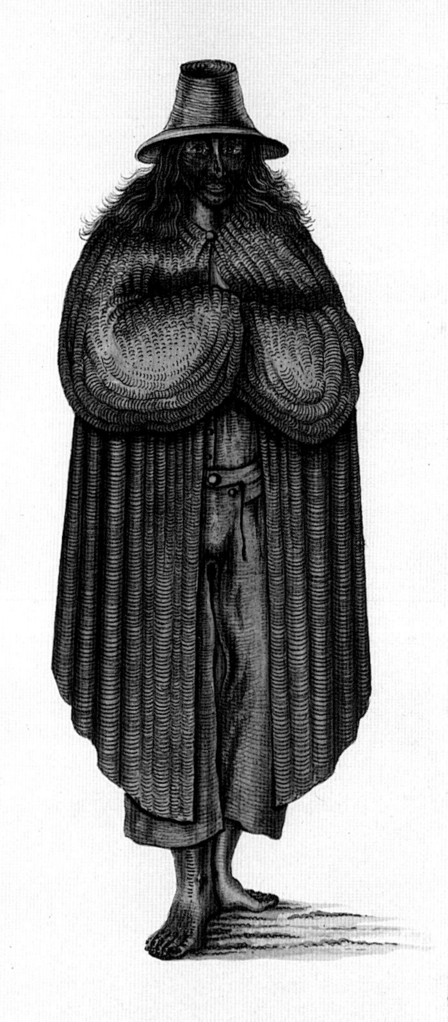

Cunnyha an Indian Chief
on the North-Side of Queen Charlotte's Island,
N. W. Coast of America.

S. Bacstrom delt
ad viv

Paul Mellon Collection, Upperville, Virginia

CUNEAH

THE NAME CUNEAH IS PROMINENT IN DIARIES, LOGS AND JOURNALS OF THE EARLY SEA OTTER TRADERS AND EXPLORERS WHO SAILED AMONG THE QUEEN CHARLOTTE ISLANDS. THESE RAIN FORESTED ISLANDS HAVE FOR SEVERAL THOUSAND YEARS BEEN HOME TO THE HAIDA PEOPLE, WHOSE CULTURE STILL FLOURISHES TODAY IN THE TOWNS OF SKIDEGATE AND MASSET.

Cuneah's town was Kiusta, on the northwest tip of Graham Island, and the first European to go ashore and visit with Chief Cuneah here was Captain Douglas, who came in June, 1789. Douglas was a trading partner of Captain Meares, and it is probable that Meares' company made the first exploration and trading contact with the Haida people. Prior to Douglas' arrival at Kiusta in 1789, Meares had met with some notable Haidas on June 20, 1784. The journal entry for that day states:

At five o'clock on the afternoon of the twentieth they dropped the bower anchor in twenty-five fathoms of water, about four miles from shore, and two from a small barren rocky island, which happened to prove the residence of a Chief, namely Blakow-Coneehaw... He came immediately on board and welcomed the arrival of the ship with a song, to which two hundred of his people formed a chorus of the most pleasing melody.

Judging from Meares' recollections, Cuneah was not wasting any time in establishing his reputation as chief of the district.

Captain Douglas built upon the earlier contact of Captain Meares by providing Cuneah and his town with naval uniforms, wash basins, kettles, frying pans and copper

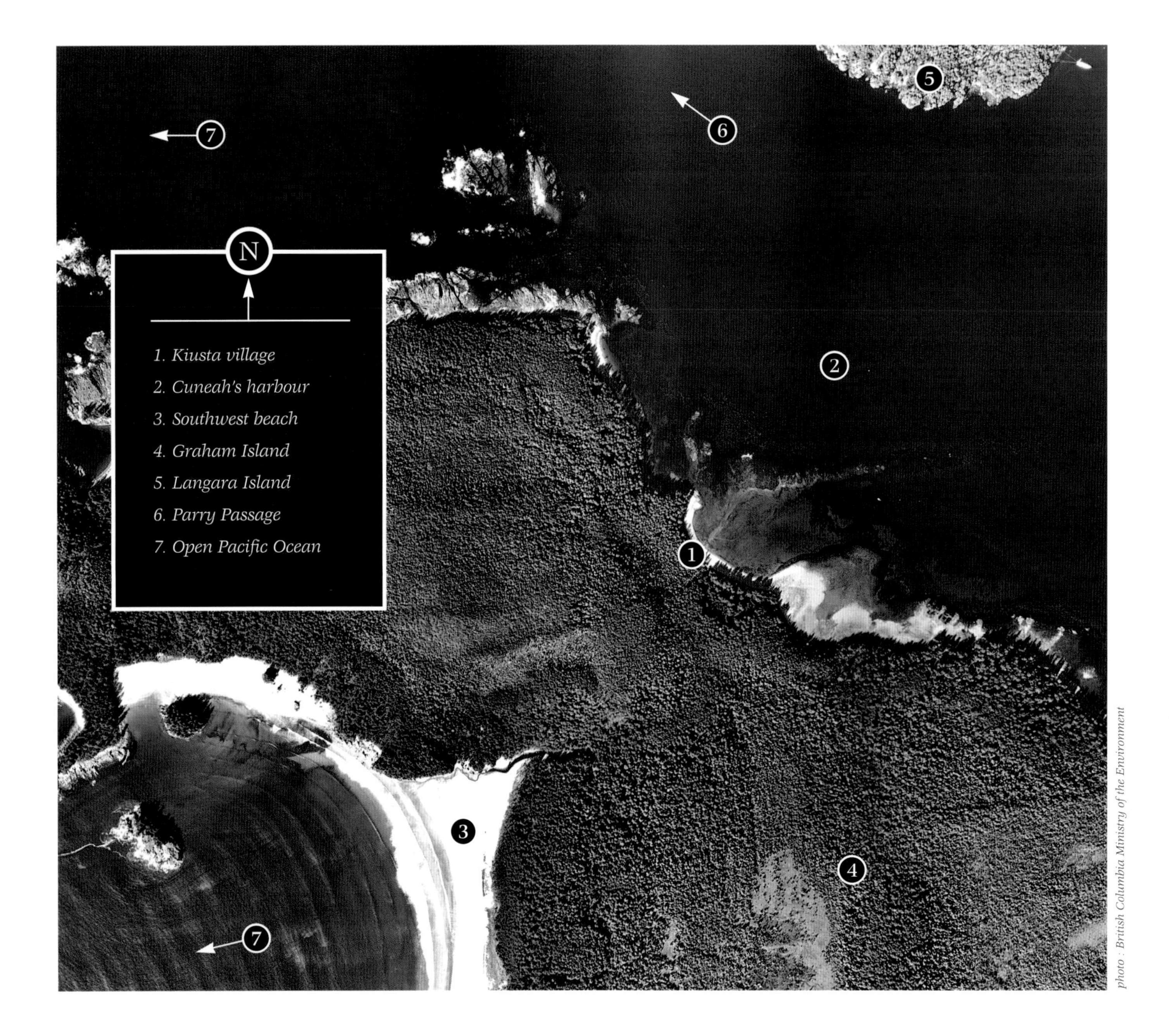

photo : British Columbia Ministry of the Environment

At left : *An aerial photo of Kiusta showing the typical twin beach aspect of many Haida villages. Cuneah's big house faced Parry Passage to the north and was connected by trail to the southwest beach.*

sheeting. In return, the people of Kiusta exchanged an undisclosed number of sea otter pelts. Besides the swapping of material goods, Cuneah and Douglas swapped names, in a gesture of Haida good will and honour — and from that day on we see references to Douglas Cuneah appearing in the log books. Whether or not Cuneah Douglas became common usage in the Meares trading company is unrecorded.

The obvious good relations resulting from this early trading visit were marred by an unfortunate incident before Douglas' group could depart. On the night of June 21 a group of Haida women slept on board ship, and a number of these ladies advised the captain that if the crew should fall asleep, the men of Kiusta would swarm aboard and cut off some heads. Douglas immediately posted gunners and guards and advised a shoot first — question later policy on any approaching canoes. Soon after the ship's lights were extinguished a canoe was seen paddling through the darkness. A volley of shot was delivered just slightly over the occupants' heads and they hurriedly put back to shore. The following morning Cuneah made a long speech of apology in Haida — from the safety of his beach. Later on he came out to the ship, as Douglas put it: "arrayed, as may be supposed, in a fashion of extraordinary ceremony, having four skins of the ermine hanging from each ear, and one from his nose." Douglas explained why the guns had been fired, and Cuneah responded, this time to his own people on the beach, from the stern deck of the sailing ship. Cuneah went on to assure Douglas that the attempted attack had been made by some of the local neighbours — people who inhabited the nearby village of what Douglas records as "Tartanee." The chief went on to add that he was now going to live alongside the ship in his great canoe for the purpose of protecting Captain Douglas and his crew, and that he had actually been the one who advised the women on board ship to warn about the danger of night attack. Douglas was impressed by Cuneah's sincerity and that night wrote in his log book that Cuneah possessed a degree of power over his tribe very superior to that of any other chief whom they had seen on the coast of America.

Kiusta's sister town, Douglas' "Tartanee," was located on the opposite side of the channel now known as Parry Passage. The Haida custom of referring to a geographic district as a chief's town often confused Captains Meares and Douglas. In 1789, the whole of Parry Passage was evidently referred to as Cuneah's town. Later ethnographic and anthropological research showed that in Haida culture, the chief of the dominant family was often called the town chief. Kiusta was Cuneah's town and logically the centre of redistribution for the chiefdom.

Tracing the activities of Cuneah between Douglas' visit and the great chief's death is made difficult by the fragmentary nature of the historic material available. However, there is another excellent journal account of events at Kiusta in June of 1789, after the departure of Douglas and his crew. This next account was written by a Mr. Haswell of the ship *Columbia*. Upon the arrival of the *Columbia*, 20 very large canoes came out to welcome the ship as she rode at anchor. The paddlers were singing "in a very agreeable air," and in a few hours over 200 skins had been purchased.

Haswell noted in his journal that Chief Cuneah was "a very good old fellow — his wife was off ship and had vast authority over every person alongside." Unfortunately

National Museums of Canada

A contemporary sketch of Kiusta village from the 1799 journal of the ship Eliza.

for ethnohistory's sake, the *Columbia* left after one day's trade, and Haswell was "grieved to leave them so soon, as it appeared to be the best place for skins that we had seen."

In a later section of the edited *Voyages of the Columbia*, a Mr. Hoskins, in one paragraph, describes the form of government he observed at Kiusta:

The government of these people appears by no means to be absolute, the chiefs having little or no command over their subjects. Cuneah, the chief of Tahtence (sic: another misunderstanding similar to that of Douglas) is acknowledged to be the greatest on the islands. His wife, of course, must be the Empress, for they are entirely subject to a petticoat government, the women in all cases taking the lead.

From Hoskins' description it would appear that while Cuneah was Town Chief, his wife had equal power in the economic sphere, being able to affirm or negate any proposal of trade.

In April of 1791, John Bartlett's ship, the *Gustavus*, anchored off Kiusta. Bartlett maintained a fine journal, making frequent references to Chief "Connehow." Very shortly after the *Gustavus* arrival, 200 or 300 canoes came out to trade with plenty of sea otter pelts. The Kiusta people wanted any objects of iron, buttons and trunks of old clothing in trade, "being very particular about this."

The following day, April 27, people began to come in large numbers "from all parts of the islands." At one time, Bartlett notes, there were about 600 canoes alongside and over 300 sea otter pelts bartered. The next morning the *Gustavus* got underway bound southward with a great many canoes following.

The *Gustavus* returned to Kiusta in June of the same year. Now most of the inhabitants of Kiusta were seen going about their daily work in red jackets. Bartlett recounts that "we knew by this that Captain Douglas had been here." And as a result of Douglas' recent visit, not a single sea otter pelt could be found for purchase. Cuneah came aboard *Gustavus* and informed her captain that most of his people had left their winter quarters at Kiusta and were now distributed among the islands for the summer.

Cuneah also told Bartlett that they did not normally return to Kiusta until the end of August. It is interesting to note that Cuneah appears to have remained in Kiusta to coordinate both the redistributional activities of the chiefdom and the public relations with the summer traders.

Before the *Gustavus* left Kiusta, Bartlett recorded the fact that the crew was becoming weary due to short rations and that they hoped to rendezvous with Captain Douglas in order to resupply the ship's stores in return for liquor which Captain Douglas needed for barter. At this point in her journey, the *Gustavus* had an incredible 1,663 sea otter pelts on board. It is known that at least 800 of these were bought at Kiusta, the winter-spring centre of Cuneah's chiefdom. From this number alone it is evident that Cuneah's town was a major sea otter pelt commerce centre for the Queen Charlottes.

Jacinto Caamano's journal gives further references to Cuneah's adept catering to the fur traders, and illustrates the Spanish ethnographic interest in the Indians of the Northwest Coast. Caamano was astonished at evidence of European and American culture at Cloak Bay in 1791. The son of "Taglus Caina" came out to Caamano's ship while she was still off the west coast of Graham Island and came aboard to act as pilot. The young Cuneah ate a large Spanish dinner, paid for it with a prime sea otter pelt, and spent the night on board after receiving Caamano's assurances that the ship would enter Cuneah's harbour the following day. Two facts are now apparent in Caamano's journal: I) in 1791 Cuneah was using the name Douglas ("Taglus") Cuneah instead of Blakow-Cuneah when speaking to the European traders, and 2) the sheltered harbour in front of Kiusta in Parry Passage was now being referred to as Cuneah's harbour.

Upon entering Cuneah's harbour from Cloak Bay the next morning, the first Haida to clamber up onto the deck was Cuneah himself. He was accompanied by two canoes containing 45 people — men, women and children. The sight of the canoes paddling towards the ship with bow paddlers beating upon large drum boxes greatly impressed Caamano. Cuneah's personal canoe was measured and found to be 53 feet long and 6 feet wide — the largest ever seen by the Spaniards.

As Cuneah was introducing himself to the ship's officers on the quarter- deck, the canoe crews were busily engaged in dressing themselves in "long frocks, coats or jumpers, trousers or loose short breeches, and pieces of cloth serving as capes of different colours, but blue predominating." Obviously, the opportunity to trade was well used to display the wardrobes bought in previous barter sessions.

While the preparatory dressing was taking place in the canoes, Cuneah's son made a formal introduction of his father to Caamano. Cuneah gently touched Caamano's face with both hands and exclaimed "bueno, bueno" as a friendly Spanish greeting. Obviously, he had met Spaniards before Caamano. After the preliminaries to trade were completed, Cuneah's daughters were called on board and shown to the captain's cabin "with a view ... to being for my pleasure." Without further ado, Cuneah piloted the frigate to a safe anchoring spot in Parry Passage while 10 or 12 canoes full of celebrants were towed astern. With the ship safely moored, Caamano entertained Cuneah and his son and daughters with dinner and music in his cabin. It gave Caamano "no little pleasure to observe Cuneah's graceful and easy manners," and in this respect "the bearing, simplicity and dignity of this fine Indian would bear comparison with the character and qualities of a respectable inhabitant of old Castile."

When formal trading began the next day, Caamano was impressed by the quality of the sea otter skins and by their fine curing. Green shells from the Spanish Mediterranean proved the most popular trade item with the people of Kiusta, followed closely by bits and pieces of Spanish clothing. Caamano was surprised to note that several of the people of Kiusta already had shells of a sort found only at Monterey. He was even more surprised when several Haidas told him that the meat had been poorly extracted from the trade shells, and should have been removed using a knife, rather than by heating, which damaged the shell enamel.

Caamano's mixture of awe and amusement is evident in his journal descriptions of Cuneah. We are told that the chief was quite short with a very strong build and a handsome face. In 1791 he appeared to Caamano to be about 70. When Cuneah came out to the ship to commence trade on the second day of Caamano's visit, he was dressed as Kiusta's public relations officer, quite divorced from his role as chief of the redistributional network of the chiefdom. He sported two sky blue frock coats, each heavily ornamented with Chinese coins. His breeches were trimmed with what appeared to be pounds of coins, and when he walked he "sounded like a carriage mule." He wore a frilled white shirt and beaver skin top hat. "At a little distance he looked very fine in his extravagant costume." While Cuneah's public relations uniform must have amused Caamano, it did not alter his opinion of the chief's dignity and authority. In Caamano's eyes Cuneah was a man who, if he had been educated and socialized in Madrid rather than Kiusta, would have belonged to the aristocratic class. The next chronological reference to Cuneah and Kiusta follows in 1793. The journal of Bernard Magee, the first officer of the *Jefferson*, records a voyage from Boston, arriving on the Northwest Coast in November of 1792. In July of 1793, the *Jefferson* anchored at Kiusta. At this date Cuneah (no doubt with ample advice and orders from his wife) had set the barter rate at one sea otter pelt per coat and trousers or, alternately, an overcoat. At this new rate only 60 pelts were obtained. Had the fixed rate been known in advance, the crew of the *Jefferson* could have traded for at least 300 pelts. As it was, for two sheets of copper weighing 60 pounds each, the crew received 12 prime pelts. The captain's sea trunk went for one sea otter pelt; there was nothing on board ship that did not have its price determined by Cuneah. The Chief was acting as Town Master in stabilizing the rate of exchange. He was uniquely organizing the redistribution of furs brought to Kiusta by the members of the chiefdom.

In late May of 1794 Magee records that "Cowe, Cuneah, Eldarge, and Skilkada, along with a number of their people, had arrived from Kaiganee with their canoes full of sea otter skins – probably 800." The Kaiganee chiefs Cowe and Skilkada had accompanied Cuneah and Eldarge back to Kiusta to trade. At this point in the voyage the *Jefferson* had 1,146 skins on board and trade goods were running low. Old sails, a Japanese flag, seal oil, the captain's spy glass, officers' trunks, flares, rockets, deep sea line, swivels and muskets were traded away by the crew. The ship's carpenter was set to work making boxes for the trade. Still more pelts were brought forth to barter.

With purchasing power approaching zero, the captain, the carpenter, and some of the crew went ashore at Kiusta "to plane and smooth a totem pole." The following day the crew of the *Jefferson* returned with booms and tackle to raise the pole into position. Cuneah, no doubt viewed with a degree of envy by Cowe, Skilkada and Eldarge, was so delighted with the crew's cooperation at the pole raising that he invited the captain and officers to a feast. At this feast Cuneah publicly thanked the officers and gave them each a prime sea otter pelt. Later Cuneah asked Captain Roberts to paint the totem pole with marine paint. Roberts was only too pleased to oblige the chief — no doubt realizing his action would earn more pelts. The ship's doctor was sent about the village to treat the sick, many of whom had unchecked venereal diseases. Captain Roberts noted in his log: "I have no doubt if we had a sufficiency of trade — cloth, thick copper, etc. — that there might be procured at this place between 1,000 and 1,500 skins." These general figures represent more skins than the *Jefferson* had been able to collect in her prior two years on the Coast. The combined total of all sea otter pelts collected at Kiusta by the *Columbia*, the *Gustavus*, the *Jefferson*, and Caamano's frigate between 1789 and 1794 is 1,600 pelts. The figure is incomplete in that it only covers four ships over a five year period; undoubtedly, many more ships collected many more pelts at Kiusta during this time span.

On July 8, 1794, Cuneah requested that Captain Roberts send some men ashore to help place "a carved toad" on top of the totem pole they had previously erected for Cuneah beside his Kiusta house. After this task had been completed, Cuneah invited the captain, the doctor and the purser to attend a potlatch that evening. Judge Howay, the late Northwest Coast historian, noted that Magee's description of this event is the earliest on record for the Haidas. Magee's account in its entirety is well worth reading:

The house was thronged with guests and spectators. The scene was then opened by the ceremony of introducing the wives of Enow and Cuneah and the candidates for incision or boring, each coming in separately and backwards from behind the screens — being saluted by a regular vocal music of all present and which had no unpleasant effect. In the same manner the presents were ushered in and displayed to the view of all present and thrown together in a heap being a profuse collection of Clamons (war garments), raccoons, and other cutsarks, comstages of both iron and copper and a variety of ornaments. This being done the spectators were dismissed and the guests placed in order round the house. The incision was then performed on the lips and noses of two grown and two small girls which ended, the distribution was then begun of the above articles, the captain receiving five sea otter skins, the other articles were distributed among the different chiefs according to their distinction after which the captain took his leave and returned on board.

Cowe, Skilkada and Eldarge may have accompanied Cuneah back to Kiusta from Kaiganee (on Prince of Wales Island) to attend this potlatch. The date of the potlatch was July 8, when Cuneah's people were normally spread out fishing, hunting and gathering among the islands. Evidently there had been some change in residence patterns between Bartlett's visit in June of 1791 and July of 1794. Not only were there many people at Kiusta for the potlatch, but there was a pole raising taking place right in the middle of the fishing season.

One final reference is made of Cuneah's continued eagerness to trade with the crew of the *Jefferson* at Kiusta. Magee, much against Captain Robert's wishes, began scheming to sell the ship's longboat for 35 pelts. Hot words with the Captain followed but in the final analysis the longboat was sold to Cuneah for his stated price. It also appears that Cuneah made the ship's carpenter an offer he could not refuse, for he and two crew members jumped ship to remain at Kiusta. The Magee journal does not record the carpenter's reason for jumping ship, but it is conceivable that Cuneah encouraged him to stay and continue to provide technical advice for totem pole raising and small ship construction.

The next chronological journal reference to Cuneah is found in the journals of the ship *Ruby*, on the Northwest Coast from 1794 to 1796. In the entry for July 27, 1795, Charles Bishop records that near Kaiganee the *Ruby* met a canoe under sail. A man in the canoe called out, "Douglas Conneeha, what's your name?" Later on in the voyage, Bishop met a Haida he recorded as "Illtadze" — this is probably the Parry Passage house chief Eldarge, mentioned by Magee in 1794. Eldarge told Bishop that Douglas

Cuneah was the Chief of the whole district (e.g., the chiefdom) and that himself and Cowe were next, but they all united under the command of "Huen Smokett Douglas Cuneah." The journal of the ship *Ruby* goes on to mention that Cowe was planning a raid on Cumshewah with 30 canoes of warriors. Chief Cumshewah, whose chiefdom was centred at Cumshewah on the east coast of Moresby Island, was clearly a major rival of Cuneah. The *Ruby's* journal further notes that Cuneah was going to visit Chief Shakes at Masset to get him to either join in the war against Cumshewah or to stand neutral.

Further mention of the hatred between Cuneah and Cumshewah is contained in B. J. Cleveland's journal of a trading voyage to the Queen Charlotte Islands in January, 1799. While about two leagues south of Rose Spit, two canoes came out to Cleveland's ship, the *Dragon*, and in one was a young man who identified himself as the son-in-law of Douglas Cuneah. Cleveland notes in his journal that "Coneyaw is head of the Tytantes tribe," further evidencing the confusion existing about Cuneah's town and the precise bounds of his chiefdom. Cuneah's son-in-law and the accompanying man told Cleveland that they were travelling south on a hostile expedition against Cumshewah's tribe, and after a brief barter session, both parties continued on their respective trips.

Cleveland's ship next stopped at Kaiganee on Prince of Wales Island. Here, "we were boarded by the celebrated chief Kow, a man whose intelligence and honest demeanor recommended him to all who had any dealings with him." The following day at noon, Cleveland's *Dragon* "arrived opposite and near to the village on North Island." A number of canoes came out to the ship, and Cuneah was the first to climb aboard. Eldarge was right behind the chief. Of Eldarge, Cleveland observed:

The latter had, a year or so ago, accidentally, it is said, caused the death of a Captain Newberry, by discharge of a pistol, which he did not know was loaded. His looks, however, were so much against him, and, in the short intercourse we had with him, his actions and manner so corresponded with his looks, that I should require the clearest evidence to be satisfied that the disaster was purely the effect of accident.

With this comment Cleveland ended his remarks about the Queen Charlottes trade, and the cutter sailed for Hawaii. It would appear that Eldarge was dependent upon Cuneah's protection for his continued life and trade with the Europeans after the Newberry incident.

A wealth of information about Douglas Cuneah is contained in John Burling's journal account of the voyage of the *Eliza*. Burling went ashore and visited Kiusta in 1799. He spent the night in Cuneah's brother's house, while the brother and heir to Cuneah's position, Chilsensish, slept aboard the *Eliza*. Burling also spent a night in Eldarge's then dilapidated village of Dadens.

In 1799 Cuneah was thought by Burling to be the oldest chief on the Coast "since the death of chief Eastgut of Chilocant up Menzies Straits." Cuneah was, according to Burling, the most respected by the neighbouring tribes to which he was known:

Indeed we have never visited a place on the coast but what we found they knew him or his tribe by woeful experience, having often made expeditions to the northward when at war, as far as Skeetkah, plundering their villages and brought off numbers of prisoners.

Captain Rowan of the *Eliza* mentioned that he had seen several girls at Kiusta that he had formally seen as far to the north as 59°, and he relates that they were now slaves to Cuneah and his family at Kiusta. It would appear that Rowan had a fair memory for female figures and faces and that Cuneah managed to capture or buy female slaves from far to the north.

Burling's entry for March 23, 1799 reveals that there were eight houses at Kiusta and two rather older ones at Dadens. Cuneah's house was the largest in Kiusta and measured 50 feet by 30 feet, rising a distance of 15 feet from the floor to the roof. At the right (west) of the village were "a number of wooden structures raised over the bodies of their dead chiefs." Burling further likened these wooden structures to gallows, noting that "some were solid square pieces of timber – about 15 feet high on which were raised the figures of men and women and children." There was a "pillar" beside Cuneah's house that had a single bear figure at the top. Both the bear and pole were painted red with ochre. The teeth, eyes, nostrils and the inside of the bear's ears were inlaid with mother-of-pearl shells. This pole is very likely the one that Magee describes being painted and raised by the crew of the ship *Jefferson* in July of 1793. It may be that the red ochre mentioned by Burling is in fact red ship's paint; the inlaid mother-of-pearl shells may be Spanish shells from Monterey.

Burling's account of his night spent in Eldarge's village of Dadens is very ethnographic. In comparing Dadens with Kiusta, Burling is rather cynical, noting that, "Altatsee's village of Tahance consists of the large number of two houses." The reception party for Burling and his host, Eldarge, consisted of "five or six women slaves who set up an extraordinary hullaballoo." Burling was very surprised to enter Eldarge's house and find 40 people crammed into its small interior space.

Eager to set Burling at ease, Eldarge stated that his people were not at all like the Cumshewahs. Here we have another instance of using the hereditary town chief's name to describe a winter village location and its people. Eldarge made the point quite clear that Cumshewah's people were his life-long enemies. The chief then made Burling an offer of three pelts for every slave brought to Dadens from Cumshewah. Eldarge stated that Cuneah would give 20 of the largest sea otter pelts at Kiusta for Cumshewah himself — dead or alive. Eldarge told Burling that it was Cumshewah who had killed the "brother" of Captain Roberts and Kendricks, and he thus deserved to be killed by the crew of the *Eliza*. Eldarge was obviously still saddled with a killer's reputation over the Newberry incident of 1798. Eldarge told Burling that killing Cumshewah would save the Kiusta people the trouble of doing it themselves. Burling learned that Cumshewah had raided Kiusta and Dadens sometime in the near past, and had killed Eldarge's mother before she could flee. Eldarge interestingly referred to this skirmish as "the time he drove us from Kiusta to Caiganee." This could possibly explain why so many people were present at the potlatch and pole raising at Kiusta in July 1794. We have already noted the irregularity of finding so many town folk present during the July hunting and fishing season. Perhaps this ceremony marked the return of Cuneah and his people to Kiusta after waiting for a time in Kaiganee after Cumshewah's attack.

It certainly seems evident that Cumshewah was Cuneah's chief rival. The ill feeling between their two chiefdoms has been mentioned as existing in 1795 when Bishop noted that Cuneah, Cowe and Eldarge were preparing to go to war with Cumshewah. Cowe is mentioned by Magee as being (along with Skilkada) a Kaiganee chief. Bishop mentions Shakes as a Masset chief allied to Cuneah. There thus seem to be three northern Haida centres of power, Kiusta and, to a lesser extent, Kaiganee and Masset, allied against Cumshewah. Kiusta forms the nucleus of the northern chiefdom that Cumshewah was trying to encompass. Here we have good historic documentation of chiefdoms feuding to enlarge their spheres of influence. From the current data, Cuneah would seem to have been successful in keeping Cumshewah at bay, at least until Burling's visit in March of 1799.

After Eldarge had spoken to Burling about his mother's death at the hands of Cumshewah's raiders, he showed him the contents of his wealth box before they went to sleep on the cedar mats. The next day Burling went back on board the *Eliza* and made preparations to go ashore again — this time to the village opposite Dadens — Kiusta. Cuneah's brother, Chilsensish, and his wife both greeted Burling on the beach, and then Chilsensish was rowed out to the *Eliza* to spend the night as a willing hostage for Burling's safe return. Obviously, a great deal of trust between the two parties did not exist at this time. Once ashore, Burling made arrangements to sleep at Chilsensish's house and then went next door to Sky's house. Sky had just returned from Kaiganee where he was displeased with a Captain Duffin's price for sea otter pelts. Lying on his back naked before the fire, Sky refused to accompany Burling to Cuneah's house, explaining that he had just dined on board the *Eliza* and would rather "lay here and sleep than go to Cuneah's."

Eventually, one of Sky's house mates who had not dined aboard the *Eliza* took Burling to Cuneah's house. When Burling entered he found Cuneah like he had found Sky, naked before a roaring fire. The old chief was ringed by a great number of nieces, nephews and grandchildren. All together, Cuneah's household numbered about 60 persons, including his slaves. Burling characterized Cuneah as being like "a patriarch of old" in this family situation. Burling was welcomed into the house by Cuneah and his wife, and was offered a large carved box to sit upon. Then "the old man told me a long story about the first vessels that visited the islands." Cuneah told Burling that Captain Douglas was the first white man to visit his part of the Queen Charlottes, and that Douglas had laid a firm basis of friendship by his kind behaviour towards the Haidas. Burling noted that "always if he is asked his name by white people he tells them it is Douglas Cuneah," and to this day "his memory is much revered among them all."

On his way back to Chilsensish's house to spend the night, Burling passed the bear totem beside Cuneah's house and noted that "it was the only thing I saw which had any idea of proportion." The difference in the tone of his journal between his night at Dadens and his night at Kiusta is very apparent. Burling had a good deal of respect for Cuneah and took some pleasure in contrasting the sagacious old town master with his domineering wife.

Cuneah's wife was a great character and most visiting Europeans, including Burling, took due note of her influence. She was especially attentive to her husband's guests, even to the point of providing female bedmates "out of her numerous seraglio with which she accommodates all vessels that stop here." Burling's own words provide an excellent description of the old woman's style:

Old Cuneah's wife is the best encourager of the consumption of rum here — regularly, before she goes home at night, she always comes on board to get drunk — and thus an object of astonishment to the whole village of Kiustah, on account of the noise she can make with her tongue; — and a dreadful plague to the old man, who dare as well defy the devil as her, when artificial fluency is added to that tongue, which is naturally so eloquent; he however has a great house for it for the forenoon of the next day, for she is obliged to sleep the whole of that to recruit her exhausted spirits and get ready for a fresh visit to the ship in the afternoon.

The last reference to the living Cuneah that I have been able to locate comes from Stephen Reynold's journal of the voyage of the *New Hazard*. The *New Hazard* stopped over in Kaiganee in April of 1811. On Sunday, May 5, "an Indian by the name of Douglas came on board, well armed with muskets, and told us that an Indian chief who was aboard last evening had suddenly died in the night." As a consequence, Reynolds felt it would not be prudent to go ashore. This reference by name gives no indication of Douglas' age, but considering that the "Taglus Conia" known to Caamano was approximately 70 in 1791, he would be 20 years older in 1811. Surely a 90 year-old Douglas Cuneah would be described as something more than "an Indian by the name of Douglas." This Douglas is perhaps the successor (brother or eldest son of Douglas Cuneah) to the title. Chilsensish is noted by Burling as being heir to Cuneah's position. Another explanation is that Douglas was a popular English name adopted by the Haida nation. In this case Douglas may be the Haida equivalent of John Smith.

When the death of Douglas Cuneah occurred is unknown. Reynolds notes that Douglas was a resident of Kaiganee. By virtue of being heir to Douglas Cuneah, Reynolds' acquaintance may be a chief of the Kaiganee Haida who moved from Kiusta. It may be that by 1811 Kiusta was no longer centre of the chiefdom. Cumshewah may have finally subdued Cuneah, or the old chief may simply have died leaving no heir.

Mention of the death of Douglas Cuneah is made in the journal of J. S. Green describing a voyage to the Northwest Coast in 1829. Green describes his experiences at Kaiganee when he tried to persuade the inhabitants to abandon their vices to become "good and happy." In his capacity as missionary, Green was endeavouring to introduce the Haidas to his God, Jehovah, "the great and good chief above, who made the sea, the land, the whites, and the Indians." Going from house to house in his zealous mood, Green discovered an elaborate cedar carving of a human head at one of the doorways. He asked his Kaiganee interpreter who was represented by the bust, and was told that it was "Douglas, a chief of this tribe, who had long since died in a drunken frolic." Upon closer examination, the bust turned out to be the lid of a burial box, and when Green peeked inside, he saw the remains of the dead chief. On the basis of Caamano's estimate of Cuneah's age in 1791, one must question whether this was the dead chief. The account of his death in "a drunken frolic" seems an unlikely demise for Cuneah; it may be that Green was disposed to believe that all Indians died in a drunken frolic, or that the old chief did indeed fall victim to the sad effects of acculturation.

It is certainly evident from Green's account that Kiusta had been abandoned before 1829, and it would seem that the abandonment could have occurred before the 1811 account of Kaiganee by Stephen Reynolds. Cuneah may indeed have moved to Kaiganee with his people prior to 1811. We know from Burling's account that Cuneah was offering 20 of the largest sea otter pelts in Kiusta for Cumsḥewah during the summer of 1799. Thus, the move to Kaiganee must have taken place between 1799 and 1811. Cumshewah's drive to expand his chiefdom, the accelerated decline in the sea otter population, and the introduced diseases of the contact period may all have influenced the retrenchment to Kaiganee from Kiusta.

When George Dawson visited Kiusta in August of 1878, he estimated that the village had been deserted for about 10 years. There were 12 houses and some carved posts still standing, "though completely surrounded by rank grass and young bushes, overgrown with moss and falling into decay." Dawson found it difficult to imagine on what account the village had been abandoned, unless from "sheer lack of inhabitants, as it seems admirably suited for the purposes of the natives." In 1878 many of the larger pieces of personal property, including boxes, troughs and other wooden and stone artifacts had not been removed from the houses. It would appear that Kiusta may have been abandoned out of fear of attack or disease. Strangely enough, Ya-Tza (or Knife Village), a few miles east of Kiusta between Parry Passage and the entrance of Virago Sound, was almost new in 1878. People from Virago Sound were abandoning their homes at this time to move to Knife Village. The chief at the new village was named Edinshaw, and he explained to Dawson that the reason for the move to the new site was to get more trade from the Indians from the north. It is also possible that the Kiusta abandonment was determined for like reasons of geographic inaccessibility and desire to draw more trade. In any case, Kiusta was no longer the centre town of the chiefdom.

The data pertaining to the wars with Cumshewah and the eventual Kiusta abandonment may be evaluated in terms of the rise and decline of Cuneah's chiefdom. During the peak of the sea otter trade, probably during the 1790s, as many as 600 canoes laden with pelts swarmed about ships in Cuneah's harbour. In 1794 we note Captain

Roberts' capitalistic lament that "there might be procured at this place between 1,000 and 1,500 skins — if we had a sufficiency of trade." At this time Douglas Cuneah was in the peak of his power — at the age of about 70. As he became older, the skirmishes with Cumshewah seemed to become more frequent, and many alien diseases were introduced to the Queen Charlottes. By 1811, Kiusta had definitely fallen from its position of prominence in the fur trade, and Douglas Cuneah was either extremely ancient or dead. His immediate successor seems to have maintained the title but to have lost the chiefdom.

The florescence of the Kiusta-based chiefdom is marked in Bishop's journal of the ship *Ruby*. Cuneah was chief of the whole district in 1795, probably signifying Kaiganee and much of the north coast of Graham Island. He was Town Master of Kiusta, and a major influence over the lives of Haidas in Dadens and Kaiganee. Eldarge, Cowe, Skilkada and Shakes were in secondary positions of power to Cuneah. Inheriting the position of Town Master and district chief was probably a difficult process for the immediate heir. Douglas Cuneah II would continue to face aggression from Cumshewah, and also have to contend with the effects of accelerating acculturation. The Kaiganee, Masset and Dadens chiefs would also have to be reckoned with during the period of title passage. The conventional expectations of the heir's lineage mates and other people of Kiusta were probably commensurate with Douglas Cuneah's fame and power. A lesser man would have difficulty filling the sky blue frock coat and top hat as well as the sea otter cloak of the deceased Town Master.

Chief Maquinna in his famous hat portraying the whale hunt. Charcoal sketch by Suría c.1791.

Photo courtesy of the Museum of New Mexico neg. no. 70636

MAQUINNA

MAQUINNA IS A WEST COAST TITLE THAT SURVIVES TODAY AT THE VILLAGE OF YUQUOT IN NOOTKA SOUND ON VANCOUVER ISLAND. THIS TITLE BELONGED TO ONE OF THE MOST POWERFUL CHIEFS ON THE NORTHWEST COAST AT THE TIME OF EUROPEAN CONTACT. MAQUINNA WAS THE GREATEST CHIEF OF THE NUU-CHAH-NULTH PEOPLE DURING THE PERIOD OF THE SEA OTTER TRADE'S FLORESCENCE.

He was likely a teenager of high rank when Captain Cook arrived in Nootka Sound in March of 1778. At this historic time the young Maquinna may have met the officers and crews of the first European ships to land on the Northwest Coast. By the time of Captain Hanna's arrival in 1785 to engage in the first commercial collection of sea otter pelts, Maquinna was launched upon his career of chiefdom expansion. His chiefdom was based in summer at Yuquot at the entrance to the Sound, and in winter at Tashees, now called Tahsis. The history of Maquinna's chiefdom is one of consolidation of gains and planned development. War, marriage with leading families, and sea otter commerce all played a part in Maquinna's program of chiefdom expansion.

Hubert Howe Bancroft's *History of the Northwest Coast* and Jose Mozino's *Noticias de Nutka* document Maquinna's reign in Nootka Sound from the arrival of Captains Meares and Douglas in 1788 (one year before they met Cuneah at Kiusta), until 1817 When Maquinna gave "a very intelligent speech" to Lieutenant Camille de Roquefeuil of the French merchant vessel *Bordelais*. From the available sources it appears evident that Maquinna was a great Nuu-chah-nulth chief for a period of more than 30 years. During this time he grew accustomed to European dinners on board ship, sleeping in well appointed cabins, and

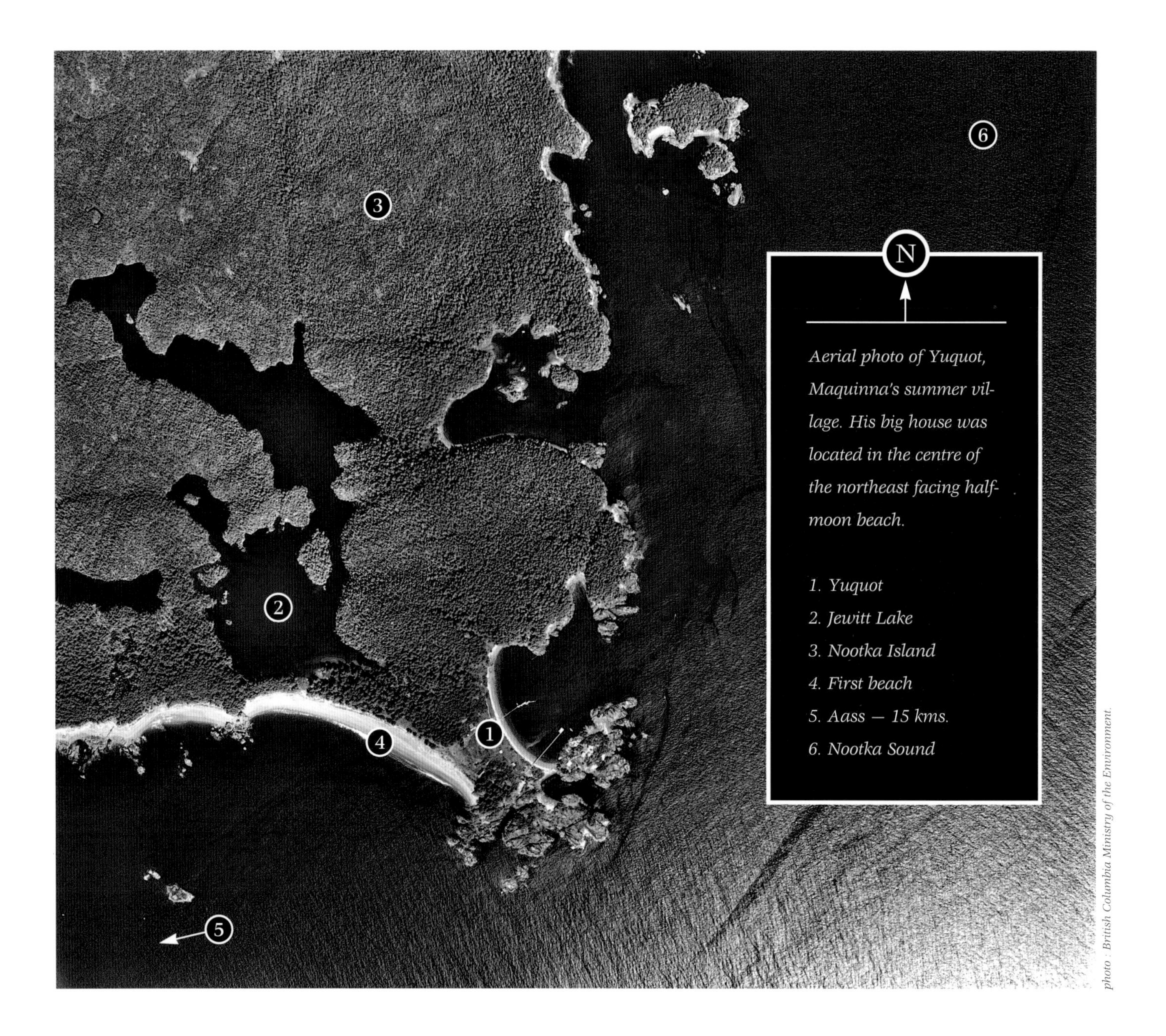

Aerial photo of Yuquot, Maquinna's summer village. His big house was located in the centre of the northeast facing half-moon beach.

1. Yuquot
2. Jewitt Lake
3. Nootka Island
4. First beach
5. Aass — 15 kms.
6. Nootka Sound

photo : British Columbia Ministry of the Environment.

wide ranging discussions in English, Spanish and French. He managed to consolidate his position of strength in Nootka Sound to become middle-man in the fur trade with the Europeans and the Americans. Maquinna was well known for his ability to drive a hard bargain, and had a reputation among the trader capitalists ranging from "an importunate and insatiable beggar" to "a generous prince." It was common practice for ships approaching Yuquot to fire a salute to Maquinna who had become accustomed to appropriate European pomp and pageantry.

Maquinna became a formidable real estate agent and resource consultant for Nootka Sound developments, selling generous plots to the American Captain Kendrick. In payment Maquinna received a swivel gun, powder and shot, 20 bolts of lace, and metal goods of all descriptions. Maquinna acted in the knowledge that the English and Spanish would always honour their pledges to keep Kendrick from enjoying his part of the exchange. To further ensure his cause, Maquinna only agreed to sign the deed with Kendrick after drafting a written guarantee of ongoing fishing, hunting and settlement privileges.

In 1789, First Pilot Don Esteban Jose Martinez took formal possession of Yuquot for Spain. Aided by his militia and six Catholic priests, Martinez tried to assert Spanish rights in the face of American, British and French trading and exploration interests. Martinez placed Captains Douglas and Colnett under arrest and seized the ships *Argonaut, Iphigenia* and *Princess Royal*. As soon as the captured British were allowed to go ashore they went to Maquinna and made an impassioned appeal for their safety. Several British seamen were wounded and the entire group complained to Maquinna about Martinez' foul treatment of prisoners of war. Meanwhile, the Spaniards had constructed a wooden stockade and were moving ships' guns to the bastions. There was no effective course of action for Maquinna to pursue, but his son-in-law, Quelquam, overcome by anger, called Martinez a pisec (wicked man). This turned out be one of the few Nuu-chah-nulth words known to Martinez, and he ordered Quelquam shot. The order was immediately carried out and his shattered body tossed overboard. Maquinna quickly gave orders for a mass move to the winter village of Tahsis. The chief himself then left for Wickaninnish's village of Yarksis to recruit a war party. Wickaninnish was Maquinna's major

At left *: View east into Nootka Sound and Bligh Island from Maquinna's village at Yuquot.*

Above *: The grassy isthmus joining the inner and outer beaches at the Yuquot village site.*

photos : George Allen

West Coast rival and this appeal for help was no doubt an embarrassing one to make. Previously Maquinna had been on fair terms with Martinez, and had promised to care for the garden, the large Christian cross the priests had erected, and even the firewood pile while the Spanish were away.

The hoped for revenge raid from Yarksis never materialized and Yuquot was deserted by Maquinna's people until April of 1790, when Martinez was recalled to Mexico by Viceroy Flores. Lieutenants Francisco, Eliza, Salvador Fidalgo, Don Pedro Alberni, and Manuel Quimper were sent to Yuquot in his place. The new Spanish delegation quickly sent word to Maquinna at Tahsis that he was welcome to return to Yuquot. Hearing that the despised Martinez had left, Maquinna returned with his people. Don Pedro Alberni realized the inhuman nature of Martinez' administration and sincerely wished to make amends. He composed a welcoming song of praise using a few West Coast words:

Macuina, Macuina, Macuina
Asco Tais hua - cas

At right : *Looking west off the sea otter reefs and kelp beds of the outer coast of Nootka Island towards Maquinna's whaling grounds. Aass village, 15 kms.up the west coast of Nootka Island from Maquinna's main summer village of Yuquot, is located on the point on the right.*

photo : George Allen

Espana, Espana, Espana
Hua - cas, Macuina Nutka

(Maquinna, Maquinna, Maquinna
Is a great prince and friend of ours.
Spain, Spain, Spain
Is a friend of Maquinna and Nootka.

The Spanish troops were taught to sing this verse to the tune of a popular Spanish song of the day, and their booming renditions echoed around Yuquot harbour. Maquinna came back at once to Yuquot and asked that the song be repeated several times so that he could memorize it. For the time being a relative calm was restored in relations with the Spaniards.

In August, 1792, the *Discovery* and the *Chatham* arrived in Nootka Sound with Captain George Vancouver in command. The British Royal Navy was on the West Coast to make final and formal claim to the area. In Europe both Spain and England were attempting to reach an agreement to prevent war breaking out between the two countries because of a conflict thousands of miles away on the

At right *: Yuquot today, showing a contemporary big house belonging to Mowachaht residents Ray and Terry Williams.*

photo : George Allen

photo : George Allen

At left *: Stained glass window in the Catholic church at Yuquot, donated by the Spanish government in 1957 to commemorate the Nootka Convention between England and Spain.*

Northwest Coast. While the terms of the Nootka Convention were being settled in Europe, Maquinna cast himself as resident host to Vancouver and the new Spanish Lieutenant, Bodego Y Quadra. Maquinna gave a tremendous potlatch-of-the-realm for both countries at his winter village of Tahsis. This potlatch may well have been the most significant ceremony of Maquinna's life. Both of his invited European chiefs came dressed in gold-braided uniforms and were surrounded by platoons of petty officers and able seamen. The arrival of the European contingents at Tahsis must have been a spectacular occasion. A colourful procession of jolly boats brought boxes of European foods, cooks to prepare them, and presents of sheet copper, blankets and beads. Vancouver's long boat came to Tahsis from Yuquot with a fife and drum corps playing martial music in the stern. Maquinna met his guests on the shingle beach and personally escorted them up to his new big house.

Vancouver described the building as an immense structure "filled with mirrors and burnished copper, brass ornaments and bright metal trinkets which reflected the glow of the central fire." After an hour of dancing to welcome the guests, Maquinna and the Europeans sat down to a banquet prepared by Spanish, English and Nuu-chah-nulth cooks and served on solid silver dishes. In front of all the people present Maquinna solemnized his friendship with Quadra and Vancouver by placing two black sea otter pelts before each captain. It was no doubt a personal blow to Maquinna that his great rival, Wickaninnish, was not present to be humbled by the entire spectacle.

Shortly after this potlatch the Nootka question was settled and Spain withdrew Quadra and his garrison to Mexico. Vancouver left for England and Maquinna was effectively divorced from his newly accustomed grandeur. There were no more dinners onboard ship and no more nights in the well appointed Spanish fort. Maquinna's days of splendor were in decline.

In the place of aristocratic naval officers came boorish fur traders with rather fixed opinions on how to conduct trade and commerce with Indians. One of many such men was Captain Tawnington, an Englishman who commanded a schooner that anchored at Yuquot during the winter of 1795. Maquinna had no reason to be suspicious

Mt. Conuma, which anchors the headwaters of Nootka Sound, as seen from the open ocean beyond Yuquot. The peak functioned as a beacon and navigational aid for canoes returning to the village from offshore whaling, trading and military expeditions. The author believes that the Conuma shape is mimicked by the famous Maquinna hat. Conuma *is the Mowachaht word for "unripe salmon berry."*

of Tawnington, and so dispatched canoes from the winter village to trade with him. The chief himself then left Nootka Sound for Yarksis to solicit another wife. As soon as the trade canoes arrived at Yuquot they were plundered by Tawnington's crew, and a number of women and old men were killed.

Shortly after this outrage Maquinna returned from Wickaninnish's chiefdom of Clayoquot Sound with his new wife. Seeing what had happened during his brief absence and remembering the actions of Martinez, the chief decided to strike quickly for revenge. Tawnington, however, did not provide Maquinna with an opportunity — he was gone on the evening tide. Unwitting Captain John Salter and the crew of the ship *Boston* were the next traders to arrive at Yuquot — at a time when none of the members of the Nootka Sound chiefdom were appreciative of a visit. The small incentive for the blood bath to follow was provided by Captain Salter when he accused Maquinna of tampering with his trade goods and lying about the trivial matter of a broken gun lock. For Maquinna this was the final insult. His warriors swarmed over the lee rail and 25 crew members, Salter included, were beheaded and displayed in a gory row on the deck of the *Boston*. Only the ship's armourer, John Jewitt, and a sail maker, John Thompson, survived the massacre. Maquinna spared Jewitt's life because of his trade. He correctly assumed that the boy, aged 20, could prove invaluable as a personal slave. Thompson's survival was a stroke of luck. He had hidden in the sail locker, and when driven from his hiding place at knife point he claimed to be the father of John Jewitt. Maquinna agreed to spare the sailor because of Jewitt's pleading that he could not work for anyone who had killed his father.

During Jewitt's period of confinement in Nootka Sound, he kept a journal that was published in New England after his escape. The *Narrative* of his adventures was published eight years later. It was ghost written by Richard Alsop and based on a series of interviews with Jewitt. The main difference between Jewitt's personal "Journal" and the published *Narrative* is one of accuracy. There is more lurid detail in the *Narrative* and factual listing in the "Journal." Alsop has substituted the romantic for the realistic in order to sell books. In the *Narrative,* Jewitt seems to enjoy the adventure much more. Perhaps, in retrospect, it all seemed much more enjoyable when Jewitt was safely back home in New England.

There are definite factual discrepancies between Jewitt's "Journal" and the *Narrative.* The major addition in the *Narrative* is the description of the raid on the Aychart village. There is no mention of this raid in Jewitt's "Journal." Once again, we must guess that Alsop wrote his version of Jewitt's experiences for a wider reading public — one that expected adventurous raids and war parties.

In spite of the hardship of enslavement in the *Narrative,* Jewitt was able to appreciate much of the Nuu-chah-nulth culture in a positive way:

For though they are a thievish race, yet I have no doubt that many of the melancholy disasters have principally arisen from the imprudent conduct of some of the captains and crews of the ships employed in this trade, in exasperating them by insulting, plundering and even killing them on light grounds.

One can base much of Jewitt's credibility as an objective reporter on comments such as these.

Jewitt gives many indications of Maquinna's political powers. After the slaughter of the crew of the *Boston,* the popular feeling was that Jewitt should be killed so that no survivors would be left to tell the story to the white authorities. The people of Yuquot feared a reprisal attack and trading repercussions. In Jewitt's words:

The king, in most determined manner opposed their wishes and to his favour am I wholly indebted for my being yet among the living.

Aside from his ability to overrule dissenters in political discussions, Maquinna was the leader of the social and religious aspects of chiefdom life. He climbed to his rooftop to direct the arrival receptions for visiting tribal delegations. His trumpet call was the signal for the men to fire the greeting volley, " . . . which they did in a most awkward and timid manner with their muskets hard pressed upon the ground." Just as most European traders fired a salute to Maquinna, the chief reciprocated in a more Nuu-chah-nulth fashion. A very important man in Maquinna's reception was Kinneclimmets, the official greeter. He also fulfilled diverse roles as public relations consultant, official dance leader, and feast buffoon. All of the Nootka Sound residents knew of Kinnneclimmets principally as a comedian. He possessed a huge inventory of dance steps and ribald songs, and could eat more herring and salmon roe at a single sitting than anyone. One of his favourite tricks was spitting mouthfuls of whale grease on the fire, causing an alarming explosion of flame and smoke.

While Maquinna had a close group of advisors from several families, the success or failure of a social or political venture generally rested on his shoulders. In his role as priest-chief, he had no control over the personal or household property of his people. He had to be self-sufficient, being in this respect no more privileged than any other person. In order to maintain respect he had to make regular gifts of food and entertainment to the residents of his chiefdom. Maquinna actually told Jewitt that if he did not redistribute his wealth in this manner he would be regarded as being no greater than a common man.

Maquinna had to amass wealth goods continually in order to maintain his rank and reputation. This task was accomplished by effectively centralizing the sea otter trade at Yuquot. Maquinna's summer village was the centre of the Nuu-chah-nulth tribal confederacy fur sale cooperative. And it is reasonable to surmise that Maquinna levied a tax for his services. The "Journal" of John Jewitt mentions that a "constant stream of traders from other villages" came to Yuquot to exchange goods.

Maquinna paid tribute to his trading partners, both Nuu-chah-nulth and European, at ritualized feasts and potlatches. On these special occasions he always sat in the seat of highest honour, and his son, Satsatsoksis (11 years old in 1803), always sat directly in front of him to illustrate his direct line of succession to his father's rank and title.

Yuquot and Tahsis feasts were ritual affairs and as such were carefully programmed. They were staged to celebrate successful whaling or war parties, or to mark religious observances. The whaling feast was the archetypal ritual meal. Each member of the whaling crew received his portion of whale meat before the non-whalers. The non-whalers received their portions of blubber in order of decreasing rank in society. Maquinna ate first; slaves ate last. Slaves actually were lucky to eat at all. When all of the legitimate free Moachaht people had received their portions, the slaves were allowed a free-for-all run to the denuded whale corpse. Any blubber remaining was theirs.

Satsatsoksis, the son and heir, performed the dance that signalled the end of the ceremonies. When the blubber distribution came to an end, dancing began beside the warming fires of the chief's house. Satsatsoksis' dance performances generally lasted about two hours, during which time his father kept time with a whistle and rattle. The other high ranking men added to the percussion section by keeping up a constant drumming. Maquinna was orchestra leader as well as choir master. He also led the chanting of the ritual songs.

The lesser chiefs and Maquinna together comprised the cabinet or corporate body of the chiefdom society. Maquinna's position could be loosely compared to that of president and chairman of the board. His opinion usually determined the peace time policy of his people. His opinion also decided, in the final analysis, the need to go to war with a rival chiefdom or to seek revenge against the Europeans. When the decision was made to go to war, the entire council organized and planned the strategy. Maquinna always struck the first blow during the attack, just as he always thrust the first harpoon in the whale hunt. If anything went wrong at war or sea it was attributed to someone acting before Maquinna had properly initiated the action.

An interesting incident of Maquinna's judgement overriding that of the entire Yuquot local group occurred when Thompson punched Satsatsoksis in the nose — a very rash act on his part! The village held a public meeting to decide on Thompson's fate. The unanimous decision of the people, including Maquinna, was that Thompson be tortured to death. Jewitt pleaded with Maquinna for mercy, saying that if "his father" was killed he could not go on living. Maquinna sympathized with Jewitt and also realized that the armourer's talent was too important to jeopardize. For this reason Maquinna asked the people to reconsider their decision. They did — and Thompson was spared.

Maquinna had a clear concept of justice, and he favoured immediate punishment. On hearing of Thompson's attack on his son he went to his sleeping compartment and loaded his gun. Had Jewitt not intercepted him, Thompson would have been summarily taken out and shot.

The office of Chief was hereditary and descended to the eldest son. If there were no male progeny the title went to the eldest brother of the deceased chief. In the regular line the eldest brother was considered the second most important male in the ruling family. All booty taken in war raids was given to Maquinna, and he in his turn redistributed most of it according to rank in a post-war potlatch. Failure to redistribute the spoils of war amongst the people would weigh heavily against Maquinna's reputation.

Maquinna explained his concept of religion to Jewitt. The

Nuu-chah-nulth cosmology centred around a supreme being named Quahootze, whom Maquinna referred to as "the great tyee in the sky." The chief revealed to Jewitt that he had no belief in an afterlife. Soon after the death of a high ranking whaler named Tootoosch, Maquinna pointed to the ground and said that was the end of Tootoosch — he was in the earth.

As priest-chief of his people, Maquinna had an appropriate role to play in the annual winter religious festival at Tahsis. This event began in December and continued for about two weeks. During this period everyone gathered in Maquinna's house to dance in celebration of the New Year. No one wore any testament of rank or wealth. The mood of the participants verged on melancholy, and the doleful singing served to further depress the emotional atmosphere. On the last day of the winter ceremonial a young boy was led to the centre of the house. Steel knives were pressed through the boy's calves and forearms and he was carried about the house suspended from the blades. After this proud rite was completed, an extravagant feast and dance was held to signal the end of the winter ritual period.

On January 15, 1803, soon after the completion of the winter ritual, there was a midnight eclipse of the moon. Maquinna went from house to house calling everyone out into the night. When they were all assembled, their priest-chief led them up onto the roof tops where everyone began to beat upon the planks. When Jewitt asked Maquinna the reason for his behaviour, he replied that a giant rock cod was trying to swallow the moon and that the noise of the beating would drive him away.

In a parallel case of meteorological phenomenon, a thunder and lightning storm, the entire village population came to Maquinna's house for guidance in the middle of the night. Once again, Maquinna ushered everyone up onto the rain slicked roof planks to drum away the evil. Maquinna beat his special hollow drum plank and sang a song imploring Quahootze not to kill the people of Yuquot. This song was soon taken up by everyone and the singing and drumming continued until the storm abated.

Maquinna directed the funerals of people in his family in his role as priest. During Jewitt's stay the young son of Maquinna's sister died and he was accorded the burial

photo : George Allen

At left : *View of the Catholic church at Yuquot from the point at the west end of First Beach.*

rites due a Ha'wil or chief. In his honour, 10 fathoms of cloth, four prime sea otter pelts, and the personal effects contained in two trunks belonging to Captain John Salter of the *Boston* were burned.

Maquinna's marriages and the marriages of those women in his family were carefully orchestrated. Jewitt mentions that most of Maquinna's nine wives were obtained from neighbouring Nootka Sound local groups. His principal wife or Arcomah was a beautiful Aitizzart girl. Another of his wives was Y-ya-tintla-no, the daughter of none other than his arch rival, Wickaninnish. Marrying the daughter of Wickaninnish was obviously a superb political move.

Maquinna was often called upon to administer medical and psychological care to his people. He treated the wound that Jewitt sustained during the battle aboard the *Boston* by bandaging his gashed forehead with a broad "tobacco-like" leaf. The patient was also prescribed regular shots of rum. Maquinna practised psychiatry in the case of his deranged brother-in-law, Tootoosch, but with little success. Tootoosch was referred to a willing Thompson for some British therapy in a last try to improve his mental health. This revolutionary treatment consisted of several brutal whippings which undoubtedly gave Tootoosch all the incentive he needed to leave this world. Maquinna could see absolutely no virtue in continuing the beatings and ordered them stopped. It would appear that Thompson, for his part, was getting more therapy out of the "treatments" than his patient.

Aside from his spiritual, medical and administrative responsibilities, Maquinna had another distinct role: leader of the whaling crews. Just as the Ha'wil was a domineering figure on the land, he dominated the Moachaht whaling parties at sea. Most of the surviving contemporary sketches of Maquinna show him wearing his conical cedar and swamp grass whaling hat. The predominant design on these hats, still made in Ahousaht and Gold River today, is the whaling hunt. Several canoes are generally depicted encircling the great sea Ha'wil, the humpback whale. In the largest canoe, standing with massive harpoon raised, is Maquinna. When the priest chief went whaling no one else would dare to strike home a harpoon before Maquinna had thrust his and made contact. Jewitt states:

It would be considered sacrilege for any of the common people to strike a whale, before he is killed, particularly if any of the chiefs should be present. (Narrative, p. 69)

To the people of Maquinna's chiefdom, the humpback whale and their chief were spiritual equals—cooperative Ha'wil of sea and land. It had always been so. As a boy, each member of the eight-man whaling crew was prepared by his father for the hunts of adulthood. When a whaler became too old and arthritic to go chasing the whales, he passed his special whaling charms on to the younger generation. The skulls of the great whalers of before were displayed in the Yuquot village whalers' shrine, and spiritual preparations for the new hunts were made amidst the bones of the ancestors. Maquinna used a four-section socketed harpoon that had been the weapon of his father. Before each hunt, a new *mytilus californianus* (the giant West Coast mussel shell) point was sharpened and fixed to the harpoon with cedar withes and spruce pitch.

The traditions of the whale hunt were as purposeful as they were ancient; harpooning a 10-ton whale required strict adherence to individual roles and perfection of equipment. To ensure that the whalers were mentally focused on their task to the exclusion of anything else, a lengthy period of sexual abstinence was required, and frequent bathing in chilly streams was enforced. When a harpoon snapped, or a canoe overturned the blame would quickly channel to the member of the whaling crew who had broken the ritual training.

Whaling technology and tradition were not part of the arts of war — they were rather acts of peace. Maquinna sang his family songs to the whales he pursued. He invited the whale to the thrust of his harpoon. Once hit and subdued, all manner of courtesies were paid the sea Ha'wil. He was invited to return to Yuquot for a princely visit — and the corpse was towed home in the manner befitting an honoured guest. As soon as the kill had been made, a smaller accompanying canoe raced on ahead to alert the villagers. Maquinna's Arcomah (highest ranking wife) rose from her sleeping compartment (where she had been in ritual seclusion) and readied the formal reception party on the beach. Young men, not yet members of the prestigious whaling crew, launched canoes and went out to help in the long arduous tow to Yuquot.

When the flotilla eventually rounded the headland and entered Yuquot harbour, a song of welcome was sung from the beach. The Arcomah was taken out in a canoe and after formally thanking the whale for coming to her husband's harpoon, she sprinkled eagle's down on its massive grey head. Maquinna and the whalers then stroked into shore and the whaling canoe was carefully carried up the beach and covered with wet cedar mats to prevent it from splitting in the sun. Next the whale was hauled as far up onto the beach as possible and roped and staked in place. Maquinna directed the apportionment of the meat and blubber. His piece was the saddle or loin portion, and each crew member had a section close to the chief's. Whale meat was then portioned out in order of decreasing rank in society. Nothing was wasted. The bone ribs became war clubs and wedges, and heavy vertebrae became canoe anchors and net weights. Of highest value was the oil rendered from the blubber and stored in kelp bulbs for ritual use — both as a condiment for meats and a theatrical explosive in the big house fires.

American Museum of Natural History

At left : *Yuquot village whalers' shrine, located on an island in Jewitt Lake (see aerial photo on page 38). The skulls of the great whalers were displayed and spiritual preparations were made amidst the bones of the ancestors.*

Understanding the vital importance of whaling to Nuu-chah-nulth chiefdom society, we can see how Maquinna valued John Jewitt's trade of blacksmith. In the spring of 1804, Maquinna put a new edge on his whaling skill – with a metal harpoon head forged by Jewitt. With this added advantage four whales were brought home to Yuquot during the whaling season. Jewitt noted that one more whale was struck by Maquinna's new harpoon and somehow escaped. Some weeks afterwards, its carcass drifted ashore about six miles north of Yuquot, almost in a state of putridity. Even so, the whale was towed home to Yuquot and ritually divided among the households.

Maquinna spent an extraordinary amount of time hunting whales. There is unfortunately no long term record of his whaling scores, but during the years that Jewitt spent at Yuquot he made the following entries in his journal:

1803

June 1: *Our chief out whaling*
16: " " " "
20: " " " "
21: " " " "
22: *Our chief out whaling, struck one and was*

near to him one day and one night, and then his line parted. Returned and was very cross.

1804

April 1: About two o'clock P.M. our chief struck a whale and killed him, about five o'clock he was towed by forty canoes into the cove. The chief was very delighted with the harpoon I had made for him.

April 25: Our chief out whaling.

29: " " " "

May 2: " " " "

31: The whaling season is now over.

1805

April 12: Struck one . . . it escaped.

15: Struck two but the harpoon draived, returned in a very bad humour.

18: Our chief out whaling; struck one but there being only one canoe fast to him, it filled, and our chief was drawn into the water, so he was obliged to cut from him.

May 4: Our chief out whaling; he is very cross because he has had no success this season. (Journal p. 109)

It is difficult to assess Maquinna's skill as a whaler from these incomplete reports for three seasons. Maquinna was, however, rather unsuccessful during these three years. It would be hard for him to maintain his hereditary rank of high prestige if all seasons were as fruitless as Jewitt's records indicate. It appears that whales were not a constant and major food source in the Yuquot diet during this period. However, when one was finally beached there would be ready food for a long time, as mature 45 foot humpbacks weigh up to 32 tons. Jewitt remarked that it was a common occurrence for an entire whale to be picked to the bones within a two week period after its capture. From remarks of this nature one can imagine that gourmandizing on whale meat was a favourite Yuquot celebration. Kinneclimmets must have been in his element during these two-week whale feasts.

Divorced from the adventurous work of whaling was the art of war. Maquinna took the Yuquot people to war to seek revenge and to gain territory. Eager to expand the geographic bounds of his chiefdom, he married the daughters of several local Ha'wil. If we are to believe the *Narrative* account of the Aychart raid, Maquinna could not brook any local challenges to his authority. The Aycharts were a relatively small group and yet Maquinna led nearly 500 men against them.

For 25 days prior to the war expedition Maquinna led the initial preparations. The warriors washed five or six times per day using spruce and briar bushes to swat the droplets off their backs. Maquinna led the men in a washing song:

Good God — let me live — not be sick — find the enemy — not fear him — find him asleep, and kill a great many of him. (Narrative, p. 21)

Predictably, no sexual intercourse was permitted the warriors during the purification ritual and certain foods were forbidden in the diet. Maquinna even approached Jewitt and Thompson before the raid, and asked them to participate in the rituals so that they could also "harden their skins against the enemy's weapons." Both declined.

Before the raid took place, Jewitt forged Maquinna a new weapon — one befitting the priest-chief's status. Maquinna's iron cheeltoolth (war club) was fashioned from a spike about six inches long and appropriately sharp. It was set at right angles to an iron handle 15 inches long, ending in a crook so that it could not be wrenched from his hand. Naturally, all of Yuquot warriors desired equally horrible weapons, but Maquinna would not allow his iron cheeltoolth to be duplicated.

When all was in readiness, Maquinna led the war party of 40 canoes on a night paddle to Aychart territory. The Ha'wil deferred the actual attack until the first light of dawn because he felt that was the time that men slept the soundest. At their leader's command, the Yuquot men beached their canoes and silently crept up the midden face and into the Aychart village. Maquinna, on hands and knees, crawled into the Aychart Ha'wil's house and knelt beside the old man's sleeping platform. With a pitched cry he drove his new cheeltoolth into his rival's forehead. At this signal the Yuquot men began their butchery. Women and children ran screaming from the houses while Aychart men stood, half asleep, and tried to fight off the surprise attack. In short order the battle was over and several scores of Aychart men lay dead or unconscious in their houses. The Yuquot men finished their work by plundering food caches and seizing young boys and girls for slaves. The triumphant war party arrived back in Yuquot the same day and a feast was held to celebrate the victory. Thompson and Jewitt had gone along on the raid, and the still vengeful old seaman had greatly distinguished himself in the fight. Seven Aychart men were killed by Thompson that day, a Yuquot record. Maquinna and the Yuquot men were amazed at Thompson's hatred for a people he had never met, and he was presented with a large section of whale meat for his efforts. The feast was highlighted by a rendition by Kinneclimmets of the entire battle, featuring fights and feints and hilarious accounts of the performer's brave deeds. The feast ended with a dance by Satsatsoksis.

Further data of Maquinna's war and trading exploits are scant. We must work from a handful of sources to flesh out a 30 year period of chiefdom development and fur trade monopoly. Captain Meares noted in 1788 that Maquinna was the "supreme tyee of Nootka Sound." Quadra, Vancouver and Jewitt provide data useful in interpreting the period 1790-1805. The final mention of Maquinna's presence in Nootka Sound is made by the French trader Camille de Roquefeuil, master of the ship *Bordelaise*, in 1817. De Roquefeuil fired a salute when his ship anchored at Yuquot and a very old Maquinna, doubled up with rheumatism, stumbled out of his house to trade. If Meares was correct in his age estimate for Maquinna in 1788 (approximately 30 years old), the great Ha'wil would be about 60 in 1817.

As in the Haida history, we find the process of acculturation to European contact ultimately frustrated the process of Maquinna's chiefdom expansion. After the bottom fell out of the sea otter trade, many merchantmen traders ceased their annual treks to the Northwest Coast. With the establishment of Fort Langley, Fort Rupert, and Fort Victoria, many Northwest Coast residents chose to spend large portions of their year at the new trade centres. The coming of Christianity also served to de-emphasize traditional Nuu-chah-nulth cultural values. And the Royal Navy began to frown upon revenge raids against rival chiefdoms. European progress in the new West Coast colony truncated the process of chiefdom expansion. Had the Europeans confined their activities to trade and the sea otter populations remained infinite, the chiefdom of Maquinna may have absorbed several surrounding chiefdoms. Nootka Sound was already under his economic and political control in 1788, and his marriages provided strong family ties with neighbouring local groups. Perhaps proto-statedom would have been the next step for his chiefdom, had conditions remained favourable. This was not the case, however, and the fledgling developments on the West Coast of Vancouver and Quadra's Island went the way of the sea otter. For Maquinna this decline in trade and prestige must have been hard to tolerate. In a period of 30 years, he had made a successful adoption of European language and custom, while at the same time remaining a Nuu-chah-nulth priest-chief. Maquinna was a great leader who dedicated his efforts to the development and expansion of his chiefdom. To the Nootka Sound Moachaht people, Maquinna was the greatest Ha'wil: priest of the winter renewal ceremonial at Tahsis, captain of the whaling crews, coordinator of local and international trade, doctor, arbitrator of local area disputes, fierce war chief, friend of the Europeans, and meteorological interventionist. No other Moachaht Ha'wil was so powerful. Even Wickaninnish at his chiefdom capital of Yarksis, far to the south, was a secondary figure. Captain Meares noted that while Wickaninnish's people were numerically superior to Maquinna's, they were a hostile, alien group by comparison. Their Ha'wil was not a man of Maquinna's calibre when it came to negotiating with the Europeans or developing his chiefdom. The title *Maquinna* and the renown it conveys, today belongs to the family of the Chief at Yuquot, now known as Friendly Cove.

LEGAIK

LEGAIK IS THE TITLE HELD BY A DYNASTY OF TSIMSHIAN PRIEST-CHIEFS WHOSE CHIEFDOM WAS CENTRED ON THE LOWER SKEENA RIVER ENCOMPASSING THE PRESENT DAY VILLAGES OF METLAKAHTLA AND PORT SIMPSON. FORTUNATELY, THERE IS A LARGE CORPUS OF RECORDED MYTH AND NARRATIVE ON THE LEGAIK DYNASTY TO SUPPLEMENT THE SCANT HISTORIC DATA RETRIEVED FROM THE JOURNALS OF GENTLEMEN ADVENTURERS, MISSIONARIES AND HUDSON'S BAY COMPANY EMPLOYEES IN THE AREA.

The primary source for reconstructing the exploits of the Legaiks is the Barbeau file, a collection of narratives compiled by Marius Barbeau for the National Museum of Man. The *Journal of John Work* for the year 1835 contains references to the Legaik who first began trade with the Hudson's Bay Company. Other important references to the activities of a specific Legaik are contained in *Metlahkatla* by missionary William Duncan, and a *Journey to Alaska in the Year 1868* by Emil Teichmann. From the outset of the Legaik research it has been clear that the three historical references refer to the exploits of two Legaiks—uncle and succeeding eldest nephew, whose Christianized name became Paul Legaik. Paul Legaik was the last great holder of the dynasty title. The Legaik mentioned by John Work in 1835 is the contact period Legaik, whose daughter married Doctor Kennedy, an official at the Fort Simpson Hudson's Bay trading post.

Prior to these two historic Legaiks, there were at least two other holders of the title. One of these men was the founder of the dynasty, the first "Chief of the Mountains" (Legaik's literal translation).

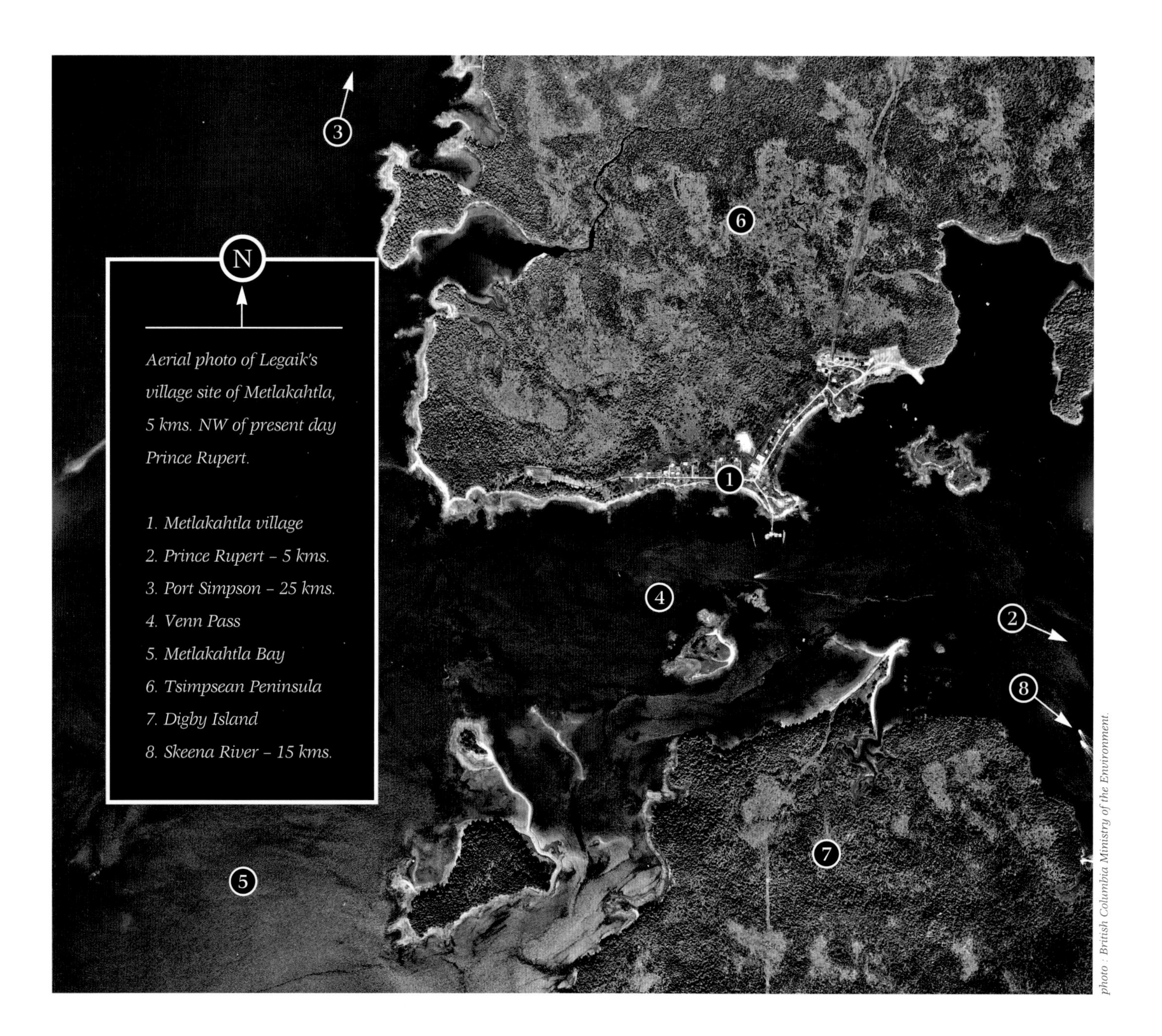

photo : British Columbia Ministry of the Environment.

As several different Tsimshian informants worked with Marius Barbeau to compile the narratives, there are often several slightly different versions of the same story. Throughout the cycle of Legaik narratives one of Dr. Barbeau's informants consistently mentioned details that the others occasionally neglected to include. Accordingly, the Enoch Maxwell version of the Legaik narratives has been selected as the most accurate version for our use.

The contributions of the Barbeau file are numerous. Based on a careful reading of the different sections, the following tentative dynasty order has been established.

Frontispiece – previous spread :
Legaik as portrayed in his Skeena River rock portrait at Tyee Point.

LEGAIK 1

Legaik 1 was the first born son of a Bella Bella chiefdom family. His mother was the daughter of Gandamalth, whose name means "taken over by trail," signifying that she had been kidnapped from a lower Skeena chiefdom and married by a high ranking Kitamaat chief of the House of Coom. When Legaik 1 reached adolescence he was told about his grandmother Gandamalth's ancestral home. Gandamalth had been a young woman of the Kispakloat House of Neyeswamak prior to her kidnapping. After learning about great uncle Neyeswamak and all of his maternal relatives in the Skeena country, the young boy decided to return to live among them and eventually take his rightful place as an heir to Neyeswamak.

Legaik's Kitamaat father, a Bella Bella chief, agreed to send his son back to his great uncle's chiefdom. Legaik's father gave him canoes and boxes of wealth goods. His mother gave him a map of the route he must travel to reach Neyeswamak's village of Metlakahtla. Several brothers and sisters accompanied Legaik on the return trip to their great uncle's chiefdom. After many days of northward travel the small entourage arrived at its destination. Neyeswamak was still alive, though a very old

man, and he realized at once the identity of his never before seen great nephew. It was at this time that Neyeswamak gave the young man the title, "Legaik," paying tribute to his hazardous and brave trek through the mountains to the land of his grandmother.

Legaik was immediately recognized as heir to Neyeswamak's position, Chief of the Eagle clan, known to the Tsimshians as the Kispakloats. Neyeswamak apparently died not long after Legaik's celebrated return, and as he had instructed, Legaik succeeded him. The young chief inherited all of Neyeswamak's property, as well as the right to receive back tribute for the wealth goods given away by Neyeswamak at his many potlatches. In addition to this newly acquired wealth, Legaik had the wealth goods he had received from his Kitamaat father. Another important source of power to the new chief were his accompanying brothers and sisters. They were also members of Neyeswamak's House and because of this held proportionately powerful positions in the Kispakloat clan at Metlakahtla. Further wealth was derived from the fees that the initiates had to pay to gain membership in the Nuhlim secret society group, of which Legaik by inheritance had become the priest-chief. For all of these reasons Legaik 1 had the power base necessary to become a great Tsimshian chief.

At left : *The wide open lower reaches of the Skeena River, gateway to the interior of the north coast. The Skeena served as Legaik's highway to territorial expansion in the east.*

photo : George Allen

LEGAIK 2

Legaik 2 succeeded his uncle, Legaik 1, who died during a raid against the Kitselas, fought to determine the right to trade with the Gitk'san. The death in battle befitted the first Legaik as he had pursued an aggressive, expansionist trading policy during his lifetime. At his death the bounds of the Kispakloat Metlakahtla chiefdom had been pushed considerably farther than their extent during Neyeswamak's lifetime. Legaik 2 was likely quite young when he inherited his uncle's title. Until the young boy reached manhood, his title was protected by a Kispakloat headman named Rhiop against slurs and challenges from other chiefs eager to expand their neighbouring chiefdoms. Rhiop became young Legaik 2's tutor and protector until he reached the age when he could properly assume the responsibilities of the title. Part of Rhiop's responsibility to his young ward included defending the Legaik title at potlatches. Several of the Barbeau file narratives describe how Rhiop purchased an enormous copper shield known as "Cormorant Copper" to re-establish the potlatch supremacy of the Legaik title. The supremacy had been temporarily lost to the Kitkatla Tsimshian chief, Tsebassa. Eager to eclipse Legaik's title while the heir was still too young to potlatch for himself, Tsebassa broke his famous "Beaver Copper" and then stacked wealth goods in front of the young Legaik until they hid him from the potlatch audience. In order to preserve the reputation and title of Legaik, Rhiop was forced to marshal nearly all of his personal material wealth to purchase "Cormorant Copper." This purchase was made out of duty and with no complaints. Tsebassa was shamed when Rhiop broke "Cormorant Copper" to reaffirm the power of Legaik.

In due time Legaik 2 came of age and began conducting the affairs of his chiefdom. Principally it seems he waged wars with adjacent chiefdoms to expand the Kispakloats' sphere of economic control. The narratives describe raids made against the Bella Bella, Legaik 1's mother's people, and the Kassan and Kaiganee Haida. As there is no mention of Europeans or European trade articles in these tales of conflict, we can assume that they were fought prior to European contact with the Kispakloats.

Enoch Maxwell told anthropolosist Barbeau that it was the nephew of the first Legaik who finally conquered the Kitselas to control trade and commerce on the upper Skeena. On this information it seems that Legaik 2 established the trade monopoly all along the Skeena — the major achievement of the Legaik dynasty in expanding the bounds of their chiefdom. Legaik 2 looms as the great warrior Legaik, and it may be that he was the chief who made first contact with the Hudson's Bay Company in the 1820s.

The Bay established their first post on the Nass in 1821. Soon afterwards, one of the daughters of Legaik married Doctor Kennedy, an official of the company, and lived with him at the first Nass trading post. By 1833 the Bay officials had decided to relocate the Nass post, and Legaik suggested that they do so on his property at Wild Rose Place. The new fort was built here and named Fort Simpson. To be near his daughter and grandchildren, Legaik moved his winter village to Fort Simpson from Metlakahtla. The date of this move is important, for the narratives reveal that the conflict with the Bella Bella and the Haida took place when Metlakahtla was still Legaik's winter town.

In his journal kept in 1835, John Work, a Hudson's Bay Company adventurer, mentions the chief Legaik "whose daughter married Doctor Kennedy." Once again, we are confronted with the politics of Northwest Coast marriages. In chiefdom societies, high ranking marriages are often conceived as an alliance between two groups, rather than just two individuals. Legaik, in engineering his daughter's wedding with a Bay Company executive, had effectively merged his Skeena enterprises with the Hudson's Bay Company. Moving his people to Fort Simpson from Metlakahtla further cemented the alliance, and provided Legaik with ready access to a market for all of the trade he had monopolized on the Skeena.

At the time John Work met Legaik, the chief was an old man with five wives to help organize his day. And Legaik was totally engrossed in courting yet another wife — a much younger girl. Work wryly noted that "Legigh verified the old adage that an old fool is the worst of fools, particularly when love is in the question." In a further reference Work stated that:

A young man, son of Legigh, the Fort Simpson chief, accompanies us to deliver a message from his father to the Kygainee Indians relative to making peace between the two tribes, which have had a misunderstanding for some time.

This journal remark may be interpreted as evidence that the nephew of Legaik 1 is indeed the Legaik known to John Work, as the battles with the Haidas took place before the establishment of Fort Simpson. In 1835 Work was of the opinion that "it is probable that they (the Tsimshian people) will not be thoroughly quiet until they be chastened and made to feel the strength and power of the whites." The Hudson's Bay Company did not appreciate the internecine raids and squabbles that punctuated much of the early history of Fort Simpson. Legaik did, nevertheless, earn the respect of the Bay personnel at Fort Simpson, and he and his wives became regular visitors to the Factor's house. They frequently ate with their in-laws, the Kennedy's, as Legaik was very interested in the welfare of his daughter and her children.

There is no reference to Legaik 2's death in the Barbeau file or in Work's journal. Work has provided the last available reference to this chief — leaving us with the picture of "an old fool in love." And then, quite suddenly, there appears a new Legaik on the Fort Simpson scene.

LEGAIK 3

Paul Legaik, the Fort Simpson Kispakloat clan chief, was very likely the third chief in the Legaik dynasty. The early effect of the Christian Missionary Society was pronounced on Paul Legaik's life. He renounced his Kispakloat clan and Nuhlim group secret society memberships after a long ideological battle with missionary William Duncan. Paul Legaik was subsequently baptized into Christianity and led a large group of newly Christian Tsimshians back to the ancestral town of Metlakahtla. Those who refused to come with William Duncan remained in Fort Simpson and continued living as Tsimshians in a progressively destabilizing social environment. The ravages of smallpox decimated the Fort Simpson population not long after the mass exodus of Christians, and many of the survivors began to seriously consider moving to the Christian community. Life in Metlakahtla was organized around Duncan's fetishes of cleanliness and the work ethic. Salmon packing, saw milling, soap manufacture, market gardening, ship building, primary schooling and compulsory church attendance eight times a week filled everyone's life. Interestingly enough, those men and women who had held hereditary family titles in Fort Simpson soon rose to positions of prominence in the Christian community. Paul Legaik became chief of the village police force, and his constables were men who had once been house chiefs. When the Bishop of Columbia paid a visit to Metlakahtla in 1863, Legaik 3, aged about 40, spoke the following words:

We must put away all our evil ways. I want to take hold of God. I believe in God the Father, My sins are too heavy. I think we have not strength of ourselves.

This state of submission to the Anglican faith had not been reached without a fight. The Barbeau file contains several narratives concerning the confrontation between Legaik 3 and Mr. Duncan. Very soon after arriving in Fort Simpson, Duncan erected a temporary church and began to accept pupils for religious training and reading classes. School days began with the missionary's spirited clanging of the school bell — a ringing event which was also repeated before each daily church service. Before too long the day at Fort Simpson was broken into periods when the bell was silent and periods when it was not. This noisy interference was not all appreciated by the Nuhlim society priest-chief, who at this time was in the community to organize the feast and amass wealth he needed to hold his daughter's naming ceremony. Duncan's bell ringing soon became intolerable. Matters nearly rose to armed conflict on his daughter's 12th birthday. A Nuhlim society feast was held to celebrate the occasion, and for the first time the young woman wore her mask and head-dress. Twelve slaves were lined up in front of Legaik's daughter while she danced and sang her own songs. Then, in the midst of the ceremony, two things happened simultaneously: a guard accidentally fired a shot which narrowly missed the young dancer, and the church bells began ringing to announce the next service. In a bellowing rage, Legaik seized a gun and shot the clumsy guard. He then stormed from his big house and ran up the hill to the church. Both the Nuhlim ceremony and the church service came abruptly to an end as the priest-chief confronted the lay-priest. Luck was with Duncan, as a recent Kispakloat convert, Taemks, interceded with a loaded pistol and threatened to shoot Legaik if he did not leave immediately. Outgunned, Legaik threw down his hastily drawn knife and walked back down the hill to his house. In prior days, no one in the chiefdom could have challenged the priest-chief's authority so flagrantly. Christianity, through Mr. Duncan's efforts, was plainly eroding the popular support so essential to the functions of redistribution and policing. The Kispakloat chiefdom was being effectively destroyed from its core at Fort Simpson.

Faced with almost daily defections from the Nuhlim group to Christianity, Legaik had to choose between continuing as priest-chief of a dying concern or making the defection himself. This decision must have been the hardest of any of the Kispakloat Tsimshians who chose baptism and Christianity. In the Bishop of Columbia's words:

Legaik was the wealthiest chief of the Tsimshians at Fort Simpson. He has lost everything—has had to give up everything by his conversion to Christianity. His house is the nicest and best situated in the village of Metlakahtla.

It would appear, however, that Legaik's cultural loss was modified somewhat by the status and relative luxuries of his new Christian life.

At right : *The model Christian village of Port Simpson in 1884.*

photo : British Columbia Archives and Records Service

photo : British Columbia Archives and Records Service

At left : *Housing at Metlakahtla in 1881. While frame and clapboard construction now dominated the village, the housing layout mimicked the placement of big houses in the previous generation.*

The next major chronological reference to Paul Legaik is contained in the journal of gentleman traveller, Emil Teichmann, whose ship stopped briefly at Fort Simpson in 1868. After inspecting the Hudson's Bay Company fort, Teichmann's shore party was introduced to Paul Legaik:

. . . who conversed with Mr. Cunningham in the Tsimpshian dialect, and had also a fair mastery of English, and his manners were far superior to those of many of the white men in these regions.

Teichmann further mentions Legaik's high reputation "amongst his own people on account of his acute intelligence." Legaik's wealth "made him known in a wide circle, and he had a great influence over other tribes, including the Indians of Fort Simpson." Over Legaik's old house at Fort Simpson was a copper plaque with an eagle engraved on it, and the following inscription:
Legaik, my crest is the Eagle, The King of the Birds, Feb. 27, 1858.

Teichmann noted that while Legaik was residing full time in Metlakahtla in 1868, his title was still called out at Fort

Simpson feasts as if he were there, and he was represented by his headman, who spoke for him and received the gifts intended for him. This eventuality parallels the period in Legaik 2's life when he was too young to potlatch for himself and was represented by Rhiop, a Kispakloat headman. Here we note the difference between the title and the man. The man may be in Metlakahtla, but the title is still in Fort Simpson. The title itself, from time to time, is held by an individual and upon his death (or disappearance) is left as an entity to be protected until it can be formally assumed by a rightful heir once again.

Before leaving Fort Simpson, Teichmann witnessed Legaik's departure for Metlakahtla:

After a long conversation with the Factor, he finally took leave, sprang with great agility into the canoe, waved us a ceremonious farewell and then lying back comfortably gave the order to start. The six short paddles struck the water with machine-like precision, and it was not without a feeling of respect for this Indian dictator that we gazed after the rapidly disappearing canoe.

At right *: William Duncan's church at Metlakahtla in 1881 : a big house fit for a God.*

photo : British Columbia Archives and Records Service

And so Paul Legaik disappears into the historic mists. There is one account of Paul Legaik's death in W. O'Neill's *My Memories of a Lifetime in British Columbia.* O'Neill remembers an old man called Paul Legaik who spent his last days in Port Simpson (as Fort Simpson came to be known). This in itself is interesting as Legaik 3 has apparently left Metlakahtla. In the latter days of the Christian settlement, the Anglican Bishop became displeased with the lay-preacher's power and ordered him recalled. Refusing this order, William Duncan instead moved his flock to New Metlakahtla in Alaska. Not all of the Metlakahtlans chose to move, however, and Paul Legaik may have stayed on and returned to Port Simpson in his declining years. There is one narrative in the Barbeau file which states that the rigid Christian life imposed by Duncan was greatly modified by those who chose to stay in Metlakahtla rather than move on to Alaska. Clan memberships were invoked once again and Tsimshian wedding and burial customs were revived. There was even an exchange of feasts with the Kispakloats of Port Simpson. Whatever the reason for staying, Paul Legaik died by drowning at Port Simpson on January 2, 1894. The Bishop of Columbia described Legaik 3 as being about 40 in 1863, and therefore the Paul Legaik of O'Neill's acquaintance would have been about 70 in 1893. Apparently the old Legaik had walked out to a reef at low tide and gone to sleep to be covered by the incoming waters. O'Neill recalls the following inscription on his tombstone:

In Memory of Chief Legaik / Died January 2, 1894 / At Port Simpson — Age 95 / Before he die he raise his eyes to the skies / and he say, Please Lord give me two hours more to live. / Four hours after he die. / The Lord gave him more than he ask for.

While O'Neill has very likely recorded the death of Paul Legaik, there is very little information on what happened to the dynasty after the move to New Metlakahtla.

LEGAIK 4

There is an Enoch Maxwell narrative in the Barbeau file which refers to the burial of the last Legaik. This narrative concerns a man who died in 1934. While this man may have been Paul Legaik's successor, there is no concrete evidence to support this theory. It is evident in the narrative that the Kispakloat population at Fort Simpson eroded to the point where it was very difficult to choose a successor to the title. A chairman was appointed to attend to the functions of Legaik as an interim measure. Once again we find the title being caretaken until it can be assumed by a rightful heir. Finally, a grandson by adoption of the deceased was chosen to become the new Legaik in 1938. The new title holder was a Gispewidwade, and not of the same family as the deceased Legaik. A successor of the same family had been sought from the other villages, but none of those approached would accept. At this point the historic and ethnographic data on the Legaik dynasty draw to a close.

Having proposed this tentative chronology of the Legaik dynasty, we can now concentrate on studying the process of chiefdom expansion that culminated in the trade monopoly on the Skeena. Our main data source will be the Barbeau file narratives. In following the Legaik dynasty's efforts to build the trade monopoly we will be observing at close hand the actual development of the chiefdom. While the ethnographic data are incomplete, and there are often six or seven variants of a single action, this examination of chiefdom expansion is based on what are probably the best available data for the entire Northwest Coast.

THE FOUNDATION PERIOD

As we have seen, when Legaik 1 inherited his great uncle Neyeswamak's position as chief of the Kispakloat (Eagle) clan at Metlakahtla he acquired a form of instant status and power. There were other great chiefs of rival chiefdoms, however, notably Tsebassa of Kitkatla and Weesaiks of Ginarhangik, who sought to check the expansion of the Kispakloat Metlakahtla chiefdom and to promote their own interests. During the foundation period of the Legaik dynasty all three chiefdoms were expanding, and their priest-chiefs were consolidating their spheres of influence. There are narratives describing the attempts of both Tsebassa and Weesaiks to discredit the title of Legaik. Tsebassa attempted to literally bury a young heir (Legaik 2) with wealth goods at a shaming potlatch. Only Rhiop's intervention with "Cormorant Copper" prevented disgrace of the title. Weesaiks sent a spy to Metlakahtla to learn Legaik's (Legaik 1 or 2) special taunting songs which bragged of the chiefdom's wealth. When the spy returned with the songs, Weesaiks invited many Tsimshian families to a house building feast and used the opportunity to sing Legaik's taunting songs against him. Against this background of neighbour chiefdom rivalry, the Legaiks created the strongest chiefdom in the Tsimshian district.

Legaik must have had a special dislike for Tsebassa for he performed one of his most original acts to shame him. It is said that for a long time Tsebassa and Legaik competed to determine who was the more powerful Nuhlim group priest. The Kispakloat narratives say that Legaik had generally been considered stronger than Tsebassa in this regard, but no decisive victory had been won. Then Tsebassa put on a spectacular performance in seemingly bringing several Nuhlim initiates back from the sky world where he had sent them. The details of this magical return are not preserved but the shame of Legaik is well remembered. In order to regain his lost prestige he sent several Kispakloat men north to the Tlingit chiefdoms with orders to find a man who looked exactly like himself. After a few months the search party returned to Metlakahtla with a man who was Legaik's exact double. The Tlingit slave was dressed in Legaik's robes and was observed by all of the uninitiated going about Legaik's tasks as priest-chief. Legaik meanwhile went into hiding.

At the appropriate time Legaik decided to hold an enormous Nuhlim society feast at Metlakahtla. Invitations were taken to several of the surrounding chiefdoms.

Tsebassa was invited to attend as guest of honour. When all the guests had assembled in Legaik's big house, the Legaik imposter performed the welcoming dance and then climbed into a specially painted cedar box. The box was then picked up and placed on the roaring fire. Amidst astonished cries of disbelief Legaik was cremated alive! Tsebassa watched in horror as Legaik's charred bones were collected and dumped into a new box. There was no room for doubt. Legaik's family began to sing mourning songs and a group of Nuhlim attendants sang Legaik's special priest chief's songs.

Suddenly from within the large new burial box came strange sounds which grew more audible until finally the lid was pushed off and Legaik emerged. He had been in it all along hidden beneath a false bottom. Tsebassa and the other chiefs present were completely shamed. Legaik had performed a master stroke and regained his lost prestige. He had shown that he had greater magical and spiritual powers than Tsebassa.

There are several narratives dealing with the first battles of the foundation period of chiefdom expansion. We have already briefly mentioned the wars with the Haida and Bella Bella thought to have been conducted by Legaik 1, or perhaps Legaik 2, prior to the move to Fort Simpson. Legaik also tried to conquer the Nishga people of the Nass River Valley. His efforts in this campaign were directed against the Kincolith chiefdom. While these stories have no bearing on the formation of the Skeena trade monopoly, they do serve to show that Legaik 1 (and perhaps 2) was interested in expanding his chiefdom into the Nass country.

In a unified series of narratives detailing the Nishga campaign, another show of Legaik's magic is described. On a supposed trading visit to Kincolith, Legaik challenged the chief, Kindzadurh, to a battle with wealth. Legaik and his men refused to beach their canoes and continued a floating dialogue with the chief from just offshore. Kindzadurh agreed to the symbolic battle and went into his house to gather wealth goods. Legaik began the contest by tossing several ceremonial coppers out of his canoe. Kindzadurh matched each of Legaik's coppers one for one, tossing his far out to sea. Next Legaik tossed several bundles of blankets out of his canoe. Kindzadurh replied with exactly the same gesture. Legaik then threw another series of coppers into the water. Kindzadurh was astonished and called upon his family to assist him. His brothers brought out their coppers and hurled them into the sea. Legaik's wife then challenged Kindzadurh's niece to more wealth disposal. The young niece had married a Haida and was rumoured to be very wealthy. To begin with, Legaik's wife threw out an array of goat horn spoons. The niece's reply to this was a large number of trade blankets. Legaik's wife had nothing else to toss overboard and taunts of shame began rising among the crowd on the beach. Legaik then called out to Kindzadurh that he would like further combat with coppers. Kindzadurh had only one copper left. Legaik dropped two into the water. Kindzadurh was finished.

Just as Legaik was preparing to toss yet another copper, a Nishga woman called out that he was using the same two coppers over and over again. They were tied to his canoe with long lengths of kelp line. Kindzadurh looked closely and saw the kelp attached to Legaik's copper. Legaik was shamed and lost no time in returning to Metlakahtla, never to challenge the Nass people again.

THE DEVELOPMENT PERIOD

Back at the Skeena chiefdom Legaik intensified his efforts to subjugate the Kitselas who lived in the narrow canyon midway up the river. It was Legaik 2 who first attacked the Kitselas village successfully and went on up-river to trade. At an unnamed upper Skeena village the Kispakloat trading party was taunted by some Kitselas traders. The Kitselas men pointed out to Legaik that just because he had raided their village when most of the warriors were away did not give him the right to trade on the upper Skeena. Legaik then returned to Kitselas to settle the question of honour. The fighting resumed again between the two groups and rapidly grew in intensity. Before the fighting had become carnage, clan brothers of both Legaik and the Kitselas chief, Gitrhawn, intervened. They argued that a peaceful arrangement could be negotiated to allow both groups to trade up-river,as the Metlakahtlans were clan brothers of the Kitselas people. A truce was declared and both groups realized their Kispakloat's brotherhood. They then agreed to exercise equal trading rights on the Skeena. There is no mention of European trade goods in the Kitselas battle narratives and we may therefore assume that these events took place prior to the arrival of the Hudson's Bay Company at Fort Simpson.

The negotiated truce between the Metlakahtlans and the Kitselas does not seem to have stood for very long. Legaik wanted to be master of all trade with the up-river Tsimshians. The Metlakahtlans began to monopolize all trade with the Gitk'san, trading herring spawn, eulachon oil and seaweed for interior furs. The Gitk'san market was seemingly inexhaustible – hundreds of elk and beaver skins were available for barter. Goat's wool for Chilkat blankets, dried soap berries and saskatoon arrow shaft wood were also traded. Once freighted to Metlakahtla, these commodities could be redistributed again at a much higher price. Legaik was in control of a captive market – and he did not relish the idea of other chiefdoms seeking a piece of the action. No other Tsimshian chiefdom besides the Kitselas was permitted to trade on the Skeena without his permission. Anyone going on a trading voyage was required to pay a wealth tax to Legaik. When any trading began, Legaik's order was always settled first. If a Metlakahtlan trader brought along a person from another chiefdom, the visitor was obliged to pay a tribute to Legaik.

Major rivals of Legaik like Tsebassa, Kindzadurh and Weesaiks cared little for the newly imposed customs regulations. Tsebassa deliberately began leading heavily armed trading parties to the Gitk'san towns. Legaik soon discovered that Tsebassa was not honouring his imposed conditions. A group of Metlakahtlan customs police were sent to intercept a Kitkatlan trading party as they made their way through the narrows at Kitselas. Legaik himself planned to lead a second attack group from down river. The Kitkatlan traders paddled right into the Kitselas trap. They were strong enough to repulse the first wave of the assault, and they retreated down river to a safe beach. Here they pulled in and began hurried construction of a defensive fort on a cliff. Logs were piled within the hastily thrown up stockade. When Legaik's second force attacked they were repulsed by a rolling wave of logs. Several Metlakahtlans were killed. Unable to dislodge the Kitkatlans, Legaik and his surviving warriors returned to Metlakahtla.

Within a short time the Kitkatla people attacked Metlakahtla. They were driven back because their arrows could not pierce the body armour and head-dresses of Legaik's men. The narratives relate that the Kitkatlan forces were near total rout when one of their headmen

photos : George Allen

Far left *: The upstream entrance to Kitselas canyon on the Skeena River.*

Near left *: The Skeena River, upriver from Kitselas canyon, near the village of Kitwanga.*

made a war club which emitted a sound like the cry of a woman. Legaik's men removed their head-dresses to look at the club and the Kitkatla warriors launched a new attack. Legaik called his men back from the fight, and made the owner of the club a large offer. The owner refused. After the negotiations for the club had taken place, the Kitkatlans withdrew from the battle and returned to their town. Their cause had been futile against Legaik's men and the matter of the magic club provided a cover for disengagement and retreat.

Just when Legaik seemed sure of a period of economic prosperity and social peace the Hagwelgyet Carrier people of the upper-most reaches of the Skeena began to rebel. The Hagwelgyet were longstanding trading partners of the Gitk'san, and they resented the balance of trade shifting in favour of the coastal chiefdom. A Hagwelgyet war party was formed to attack a Metlakahtlan trading party. When the trade with the Gitk'san had ended the Hagwelgyet attacked. The Metlakahtlans ran for their canoes after realizing that they were outnumbered. After paddling some distance downstream the men noticed that a canoe carrying some of the women from Legaik's house was missing.

Thinking the women had been kidnapped, the Metlakahtlan traders stopped at Gitenmaks and purchased guns, ammunition and whisky from the local store (and thus this is a post-contact event, likely occurring after the establishment of Fort Simpson in 1823). Suitably armed, the men returned to the Bulkley River and surprised the Hagwelgyet. The Metlakahtlan party now far outpowered the enemy's arsenal. However, seeing the opposition had only a few guns, Legaik's men opted to fight with their knives. The Metlakahtlans won the knife fight and enslaved some Hagwelgyet women. Ironically enough, the missing women from Legaik's house were found hiding in a safe spot on the river when the victors began their trip back home. They had never been captured.

Even after the Hudson's Bay Company established themselves on Legaik's property, the Kitkatlan people continued to trade with the Gitk'san and Hagwelgyet. Legaik soon adopted a new punitive strategy. He decided to raid the upper Skeena towns of his chiefdom rather than the Kitkatlan smugglers who were trading with them. The priest-chief led a war party past all of the lower towns without attacking, for he had decided to strike the Kispiox people first. As the Metlakahtlan canoes approached many of the Kispiox people ran off into the forest. Legaik then lured them back by opening and closing a large umbrella that he had bought at the Bay. While dancing and opening the umbrella, Legaik sang a Nuhlim song about the strange object's supernatural powers. The Kispiox people were tricked into thinking that Legaik had come up river to show them his new magical possession. A feast was quickly arranged to celebrate the arrival of the chiefdom's head. During this feast Legaik's men attacked the Kispiox and burned the village to the ground. The next morning Legaik set off for Gitenmaks, Gitsegyukla and Kitwanga. News of his approach preceded the war party, and by the time they arrived each town was deserted. Finding only house posts and rafters left, Legaik had to be content with burning them.

After destroying what remained of Kitwanga, Legaik moved back down river to Kitselas canyon. Fully expecting this eventuality, the Kitselas had fortified their village with heavy logs. When Legaik and his men tried to attack the cliff-top town they were repulsed by a sea of rolling logs. Realizing the futility of continually attempting to storm the

Right *: Tsimshian Eagle Pole at Kispiox, Skeena River, as recorded by the artist Emily Carr in 1912.*

British Columbia Archives & Records Service (PDP00599)

rock face, Legaik led his troops to one side of the cliff where it was not so steep. Here the warriors each put on a special head-dress designed by Legaik which looked exactly like the hips of a woman. The Kitselas were so distracted by these hip symbols that the Metlakahtlans were able to storm the fort. Before hand to hand fighting could begin, Neestarhoik, a visiting Gispewidwade chief, intervened and managed to negotiate a settlement.

Finally, Legaik had subdued all of the towns that formed the interior settlements of his chiefdom. Now he was popularly acknowledged as being the highest ranking Tsimshian priest-chief. However, the other chiefdom heads were still angry at the arrogance of his displays of power. An unprecedented meeting of chiefdom councils was held at which it was decided to annihilate Legaik and all of his town folk. By destroying the centre of his chiefdom they hoped to collapse the empire. Many of the council members at the meeting were married to women of Legaik's family and they were sworn to keep the raid a secret. Fortunately for the Metlakahtlans, several men could not bear the thought of killing their own relations, and word of the attack was leaked to Legaik.

After consulting with his headmen, Legaik sent a challenge to all the chiefs of the coastal Tsimshian chiefdoms in opposition to his trade monopoly. He challenged them first to fight with wealth, then with slaves, and then with coppers. If he should lose the challenge, the Metlakahtlans would agree to fight against all the rest.

Legaik waited three weeks and the other chiefs did not accept his challenge. Accordingly he gave a huge feast for his town to celebrate the victory by acclamation. During their victory feast Legaik announced that he would hold the biggest potlatch of his life, at which time he would give away coppers to the chiefs of the other Tsimshian chiefdoms. The potlatch was staged without further conflict, and it is said that over 30 canoe loads of people came to the great feast.

Ten days afterwards, Legaik called his headmen together and announced that he planned to have his face, along with the ceremonial coppers that he had given away, immortalized in paint upon a mountain. The site selected was Tyee Point, a prominent rock face on the Skeena trade route used by all the Tsimshian people. Lequate, of the Gitsees, was commissioned to paint the rock mural. While all the trade parties were away at the Nass, Lequate was suspended,in a basket made of cedar limbs, from the top of the sheer cliff to paint the rock mural. When finished, the rock portrait symbolized Legaik's control of all trade on the Skeena. While hidden from today's main C.N.R. trade route and highway, the Legaik pictograph still survives in remarkable condition as a continuing tribute to an extraordinary period of Tsimshian history.

It is a tribute to the status of the dynasty that the name of Legaik is still remembered and spoken of by present day Tsimshian people, especially in the Prince Rupert area.

References for Further Reading

Bancroft, H.H. (1884). *History of the Northwest Coast.* A.L. Bancroft and Co. Publishers, San Francisco.

Bartlett, J. (1925). "John Bartlett's Narrative", in *The Sea, The Ship and The Sailor,* Marine Research Society, Salem, Massachusetts.

Bishop, C. (1794-1976). *Commercial Journal of the Ship Ruby.* Original in B. C. Archives, Victoria.

Burling, J. (1799). *Journal of the Eliza.* Photostat of original in U.B.C. Special Collections (mistakenly attributed to William Sturgis).

Cleveland, R.J. (1805). *In the Forecastle or Twenty-five Years a Sailor.* Hurst and Co. Publishers, New York.

Dawson, G.H. (1880). *Geological Survey of Canada: Report on the Queen Charlotte Islands.* Queen's Printer, Ottawa.

Drucker, P. (1951). *The Northern and Central Nootkan Tribes.* U.S. Government Printing Office for Bureau of American Ethnology (Bulletin 144), Washington, D.C.

Drucker, P. (1965). *Cultures of the North Pacific Coast.* Chandler Publishing Co., San Francisco.

Duncan, W. (1889). *Metlakatlah.* Church Missionary Society, London.

Green, J.S. (1915). *Journal of a Tour on the Northwest Coast of America in the Year 1829.* Chas. Heartman, New York. Copy of original in B. C. Archives, Victoria.

Haswell, R. (1789). *A Voyage Around the World on Board the Ship Columbia Rediviva and Sloop Washington in 1787-89.* Typed copy of original in B. C. Archives, Victorla.

Howay, F.W. (ed.) (1941). *Voyages of the Columbia to the Northwest Coast 1787-1790 and 1790-1793.* The Massachusetts Historical Society, Boston. (Copy of the original in B. C. Archives, Victoria).

Howay, F.W. (ed.) (1942). "A Yankee Trader on the Northwest Coast, 1791-1795," in *The Washington Historical Quarterly*, Vol. 21. Washington University State Historical Society. Copy of Original in B. C. Archives, Victoria.

Jewitt, J.R. (1896). *Narrative of the Adventures and Sufferings of John R. Jewitt.* London.

Jewitt. J. (l931) *A Journal Kept at Nootka Sound,* Goodspeed Press, Boston.

McKelvie, B.A. (1946). *Maquinna the Magnificent.* Southam Press, Montreal.

Meares, J. (1790). *Voyages Made in the Years 1788 and 1789, from China to the NorthWest Coast of America*. Logographic Press, London.

Menzies, A. (1923). *Journal of Vancouver's Voyage, April to October.* B. C. Archives Publication, Victoria.

Mozino, J. (trans. I.R. Wilson) (1970). *Noticias de Nutka*. McClelland and Stewart, Toronto.

O'Neill, W. (1964). *My Memories: A Lifetime in British Columbia*. Original in B. C. Archives, Victoria.

Reynolds, S. (1811). *The Voyage of the New Hazard.* Copy of the original manuscript in B. C. Archives, Victoria.

Rosman, A. and Rubel, P.G. (1971). *Feasting with Mine Enemy: Rank and Exchange Among Northwest Coast Societies.* Columbia University Press, New York.

Service, E.R. (1962). *Primitive Social Organization; An Evolutionary Perspective.* Random House, New York.

Swanton, J.R. (1905). *Contributions to the Ethnology of the Haida.* Leiden, E.J. Brill Ltd., New York.

Teichman, E. (1963). *A Journey to Alaska in the Year 1868: Being a Diary of the Late Emil Teichman.* New York.

Tolmie, W. *Diary for 1834*. Copy of original in the U.B.C. Special Collections Division.

Wagner, H.R. and Newcombe, W.A. (1938). "The Journal of Jacinto Caamano," in *B. C. Historical Quarterly,* July. Victoria.

Work, J. (1823). *The Journal of John Work.* Copy of original in B. C. Archives, Victoria.

Mahood, I.S. (1971). *The Land of Maquinna*. Agency Press Ltd., Vancouver.

Acknowledgements

Sea Otter Chiefs was first written as an Honours Anthropology thesis for professor Wilson Duff at the University of British Columbia in 1973. Rather than following Professor Duff's advice and continuing Anthropology, the author studied Law instead. To combat the boredom of contract and tax classes in 1976 he re-wrote the thesis in more popular language and *Sea Otter Chiefs* was first published by Friendly Cove Press in 1978. It sold out and has been unavailable ever since. This much enhanced new edition owes its genesis to the constant, kind and welcome prodding of Geoff and Frankie Robinson, Myrna and Jim Boulding, Bill and Dave Ellis, Karen Cooke and Tim McDaniels,Lynn Webster and Caitlin and Lance Robinson.

A special thank you is due Ashis Gupta and George Allen of Bayeux Arts Incorporated who agreed to take the entrepreneurial risk and publish the book. Canadian authors salute your courage!

A final note of thanks is extended to the Sea Otter Chiefs themselves; their collective spirit lives on in the First Nations of the Northwest Coast.

Dedication

Over the past twenty years the author and his family have developed an enduring friendship with Terry and Ray Williams and their family at Yuquot. Terry and Ray are exemplars of *generosity of spirit,* the Mowachaht way, and the power of the human will. When the Mowachaht were convinced by the Department of Indian and Northern Affairs to leave Yuquot for Gold River in 1967, Terry and Ray stayed on. They keep their language alive, sing the old songs, steward the lands and seas of their chief and show the world that acting locally and thinking globally is possible. Their example is an inspiration to all west coasters. Wocash!